T0307196

PLEASE DON'T TAKE ME HOME

PLEASE DON'T TAKE ME HOME

A LOVE STORY WITH FULHAM FOOTBALL CLUB

SIMONE ABITANTE

First published by Pitch Publishing, 2022

Pitch Publishing
A2 Yeoman Gate
Yeoman Way
Worthing
Sussex
BN13 3QZ
www.pitchpublishing.co.uk
info@pitchpublishing.co.uk

ISBN 978 1 80150 065 4

Typesetting and origination by Pitch Publishing
Printed and bound in Great Britain by TJ Books, Padstow

Contents

This book is dedicated to the loving memory of my dear friends Umberto Scomparin and Giampaolo Bonato, who both departed this world too early. They taught me what true friendship means and that will stay with me forever. Their passion for football was second only to their love for life.

To friends, to love, to vodka ...

Why Fulham?

Soundtrack: 'The Rhythm of the Night' –
Corona

BEING AN Italian in London, I got used to this question when declaring my love of the Whites of west London, 'Why Fulham?'

People, even nowadays, keep asking me why I support Fulham.

People, even nowadays, keep receiving the same answers. The easiest one is simple, 'Why not?'

The more romantic one, 'Because it's like love and most of the time there's no explanation, it happens, that's it.'

Got it?

My true, passionate, berserk, total love for Fulham FC kicked off between 2000 and 2001 when I was a full-testosterone, adrenaline-charged young Italian guy moving to London from a little village in the north of Italy.

Before talking about it though, let's rewind back a little because a strong feeling like the one I developed for Fulham is something that goes beyond compare and logic and needs explanation.

Being born on 1 November 1975, I was not even seven when the Azzurri claimed an important part in my future life when winning the 1982 World Cup. I still have clearer memories of those games than other much more recent ones. I know the starting XI by heart and pictures of what happened are printed forever in my mind: Paolo Rossi nicking goals in the box, Marco Tardelli's iconic screaming celebration after netting in the final, Maradona's shirt trashed by a young badass in the making, Claudio 'Gheddafi' Gentile[1], the perfect example of when your destiny is not in your surname.

That same summer a certain Michel Platini signed for Juventus and I became a Bianconero. In a black-and-white-striped shirt, with the magic number ten on the back, he resembled my life dream. I had found a favourite player and Juventus was my chosen team.

As a kid I was playing football every day. I quickly joined the club of 'who broke a window with a ball at least once in his life' and quickly after also another one, less desired, 'who broke a bone playing football'. Ouch!

My uncle then took me to a football ground for the very first time. I'm from Vicenza and Lanerossi Vicenza in the mid-1980s were still a very respectable club, playing in Serie A. During the late 70s they were even nicknamed 'Real Vicenza', finishing second, behind Juventus and 'our' Paolo Rossi being crowned top scorer. When he died in December 2020, his funeral was held in Vicenza's main dome.

The city's ground is dedicated to former player Romeo Menti, who died in the Superga disaster on 4 May 1949 when the aeroplane flying back Torino FC's players and staff crashed on the hills of the city of Turin.

I love our stadium because it's quite English. It's built right in the city, surrounded by houses and inside you're close to the pitch. Its capacity is around 20,000 and the atmosphere has always been great.

---

1 Gentile in Italian means gentle

In Vicenza we're very passionate about football. In the 2019/20 season, with the club in the third tier, there were 8,000 season ticket holders!

Back to my uncle, and at the time he was also a season ticket holder but a quiet one who used to sit in the side stand. He was not a terrace man, let's put it like that.

My brother though, 13 years my senior, actually liked being in the crowd of the *Curva Sud*, what in England would be called the South Terrace or South End. So, together with his friends, one Sunday, the day of football in Italy before the pay-per-view puzzle, they grabbed this young football fanatic and took him again to the Stadio Romeo Menti in Vicenza.

Those days you could get a cheaper ticket to the *parterre*, similar to a lower end, and then be helped up to the upper end in the actual *Curva Sud* where the hardcore fans used to be.

That was amazing and crazy at the same time for me; thousands singing, shouting, smoke flares, huge flags, scarves, a couple of guys playing drums, and it looked to me like a nice party. Booze and joints completed the picture but at the time I had to be told what they actually were. I totally loved the experience and wanted more.

The excitement was superb and for a little boy aged 11 in an era where PlayStation, internet and social media were far away from people's imagination, being taken to a game was luxury.

I went again with my uncle and I'll be always thankful to him for that, but remaining seated on the family-packed side of the pitch was simply not for me.

Instead, I wanted to be up there standing, jumping around singing, actively supporting my team among my friends, getting behind the players with all my voice, disregarding the weather conditions.

That wish came true when my great friend Mirko asked me to join him and his uncles, God save the uncles, in getting a season ticket. We were 16 by then and thankfully my mum agreed with it. That was 1991 and the under-18 season ticket cost me something like £80, a bargain.

Those were also the days I discovered English football and the then-called First Division, soon to become the Premier League. Peter Schmeichel was a Manchester United player as was a young Ryan Giggs. Vinnie Jones wore Chelsea colours in mid-table and the red and white Arsenal got my early sympathies while the John Fashanu myth started up here in Italy thanks to a TV show called *Mai dire Gol*[2].

During the mid-1990s most of the world's best footballers were playing in Serie A, which was also the most watched league in the world. Juventus won their last Champions League in 1996 while the English Premier League was growing fast.

And the mid-90s were also the most successful years in Vicenza's football history.

After being promoted to Serie B in 1993, only two years later they got back to Serie A and finished in an extraordinary ninth place. The following season, 1996/97, was incredible. In the opening game Vicenza won 4-2 away to a Fiorentina team managed by Claudio Ranieri and including Gabriel Batistuta, Rui Costa, Francesco Toldo and Luís Oliveira. By the end of November they were even topping the Serie A table.

Impressive performances also saw them beat Juventus, Inter Milan and AC Milan on the way, improving on the remarkable achievement of the previous season by ending up in eighth.

That would have been enough for club and supporters but the icing on the cake arrived at the end of May when, at home, they beat Napoli 3-0 to win their very first Italian Cup 3-1 on aggregate. A fantastic achievement for the *Noble Provincial* as the club was often called.

---

2   Never say goal

I was there and that was mental. We invaded the pitch at the final whistle and were celebrating together with the players after that totally unpredictable trophy win.

It was one of the best nights of my life, and carousels of cars shortly followed through the city streets and even the police got nicer. As I was waving my own red and white flag with my upper body outside the car window while controlling the pedals with my feet, my mate actually managed the steering wheel from the passenger seat. 'Hey, genius, get inside your car, now,' they scolded me. It all ended with some blushed cheeks and a loud laugh from the three of us.

That win meant Europe the following season and Vicenza enjoyed another memorable campaign, getting to the semi-finals of the old European Cup Winners' Cup and making a name for themselves even outside Italy.

Unfortunately it ended in tears. After beating Chelsea 1-0 at home, Vicenza went one up at Stamford Bridge and scored a second goal, which would have definitely been enough, only for it to be ruled out for a non-existing offside. That was it; the star-studded Blues came back with Poyet and Zola, the Magic Box, with a certain Mark Hughes scoring the fatal third goal towards the end. A usually average Ed de Goey was Chelsea's saviour in both games.

Now you know when my sporting hate for the other team in Fulham began.

I often go back to that game thinking about the what ifs. Chelsea played Stuttgart in the final, although many pundits at the time said Vicenza–Chelsea was the real final as the Blues had a very strong team and Vicenza were playing an incredible fear-nothing, attacking style of football.

My First London

Soundtrack: 'Babylon' – David Gray

WHEN AT the end of November 2000 my pal Marco and I decided to eventually move to London and meet up with Umberto, a great friend from Italy already living there, Vicenza had gone down but had immediately bounced back to Serie A. Lazio were the reigning champions after beating Juventus by just one point thanks to the infamous Perugian rainy defeat while in England, Manchester United had won their 13th title with Sunderland's Kevin Phillips bagging 30 goals and the Golden Boot.

On the way to our friend's house in Tooting Bec, his car broke down so our first task on English soil was to get familiar with the famous London Underground. The iconic tube map looked like an intricate electric scheme to me, only coloured.

Umberto briefly told us what to look for and where to change to get the black line heading south. I recall staring for at least ten minutes at those packed trains, impossibly overcrowded by people from at least 30 different countries.

Mind you, I was coming from a village where everybody knows each other and the most exotic faces had been a family moving there from Naples, together with the odd Albanian builder or Moroccan door-to-door carpet seller.

With all the money I had, around two million Italian lire, safely hidden next to the 'family jewels', we squeezed into the train for Morden. Once arrived in Tooting Bec, we got on to the street and the first sight was a bunch of thugs in hoodies and worn-out trainers playing around a parked car probably trying to steal something from it. Welcome to the real world, Simone!

The houses, the old pubs, London's famous grey sky, I loved everything.

Adjusting to life in a metropolis like London took me more or less a month. I changed three jobs as a young waiter-in-the-making with semi-decent English, and as many houses.

At the time I remember 10,000 Italian lire, enough back home for a good pizza and a drink, being short even for a meal at McDonald's. One English pound equated to nearly 3,500 lire.

It was tough but at least I could have fun like a kid at Christmas every time I wanted just by walking into the Tower Records in Piccadilly Circus, which was heaven for a music lover like me!

Towards New Year's Eve I eventually had a proper full-time job in a small restaurant in Hampstead and was sharing a room with my mate and a new Italian friend in a not-so-flashy hostel in Royal Oak. Welcome stability gave me time to realise that I needed an English team to support.

London had plenty to choose from. I sympathised for Arsenal, Chelsea were not an option, and Spurs neither as the ENIC group which bought Vicenza a couple of years before, dismantling a successful team, were on the verge of acquiring Spurs and I didn't want anything to do again with them.

Outside the capital city I liked Manchester United as abroad it was easier to get to know the big teams rather than others. Being a Juventus fan, the Heysel memory was still strong so I couldn't go for Liverpool. Everton were their rivals so they could also be an option. I liked the name and history of Nottingham Forest, and I looked for teams wearing red-and-white-striped kits so Sheffield United, Sunderland, Stoke got into the raffle.

Back to London there were also West Ham, and QPR who were famous in Italy for their jersey. I decided I didn't want to support a big team, I wanted an underdog.

Then one day I recall being on the tube getting to work, as usual picking up the *Metro* paper to give it a look. There was a nice article talking about this black and white team taking the First Division by storm. I was curious.

I found out from those pages that Jean Tigana was the manager; I remembered liking him playing alongside my idol Platini in the French national team. I had to know more.

My room-mates were both working at the Teca Restaurant just off Bond Street Station, and as I used to finish earlier than Davide and Marco I was often going there to see them, having a beer at the bar and waiting for them so we could go home together. It was early on in the days of the internet so sometimes we would go to the Easy Internet Café to browse for £1 before going home. It was there that I looked for more info about this Fulham Football Club. I saw they were doing really well, they had some good footballers in the likes of Louis Saha, Barry Hayles, John Collins and Bjarne Goldbaek, and I already knew Karl-Heinz Riedle from his Italian days. I liked the fact they wore black and white like Juventus and when I read that one of their biggest rivalries was with Chelsea I knew it had to be them.

I was happy; I had my English team to support and also I could possibly watch live with Fulham being in London.

Living in London was great and every time I was going back home I was received almost like a celebrity, and yes, it worked well with the girls.

Although a hostel is not the most respectable place on earth, I have hundreds of stories about the one we were living in.

Once, I got back and found somebody sleeping in my bed. Me and my friend had paid a little extra to stay in a three-person room with the promise of it being just the two of us. As I opened the door the mixed smell of booze and sweat punched me straight in the stomach, so just imagine how I would react seeing this figure, still dressed and with his muddy Timberlands on, resting in my clean bedsheets, all my clothes on the floor.

I got mental; I was shaking this guy shouting at him, 'What the fuck are you doing in my bed? Who are you?' No reply; I reckon he'd passed out.

Then later on, after calming down in some friends' room, I went back there. He was on the top bed, still dressed and dirty. He turned and whispered, 'You can take your bed now, is warm.' I wanted to kill him.

And I think I was not the only one because when he came back to this world, he showed us a huge cut going from his chest down to his belly. He said that was the reason why he ran away from his previous place. The guy was French-Turkish and he had just run from a complicated situation, he said. The day after, he got a different room.

Then, when me and Marco moved to the room where Davide was, to be the three of us, we could hear 'Smells Like Teen Spirit' being played 24 hours a day next door. This went on for all of our stay. Nobody had ever seen who was renting that room and the Nirvana song kept us company all the time.

Unfortunately, working in the restaurant business most of the time meant working weekends. My day off was on Monday and I used to spend the morning in bed until late then go into the centre, listening to some new CDs at Tower Records, eating at KFC or in one of the Chinese restaurants near Leicester

Square, or scouting Camden Town's alleys for The Cure's or Joy Division's memorabilia and gadgets.

Later on in the afternoon I'd move to the arcade in Goodge Street and spend a few hours giving *Virtua Striker* lessons to some random Japanese guys.

Yup, all video games were Sega or Atari, but when we talk about football, there's never been so much of a game between Italy and Japan.

So, after my £1 coin lasted for hours it was time to move next door to an Italian café which had a huge room downstairs and was showing live Italian games with an Italian commentary.

My mouth is still watering remembering the amazing sandwiches they used to serve, using imported Italian products which made me feel at home.

Looking back, it reminds me of some movies when Italian immigrants gather together, smoke heavily, talk loudly and move arms and hands in the air frequently.

The year 2001 was a year of mixed feelings for me both life- and football-wise.

My mates decided to go back to Italy around Easter time. I was earning good money, my English was improving, and I loved London albeit at work my female manager was giving me a hard time – yes, harassment can be both sides – I decided to stay.

In football, once again Juventus were second, this time to Roma, the Italian capital city celebrating two titles in a row. Then the worst development – Vicenza were relegated on the last day of the season. It was sad to accept, and as a fan you could see the golden years were fading away; the new ownership – Vicenza were the very first Italian club owned by a foreign property – seemed not to care much about our proud history and looked only focused on taking advantage financially of what the team had achieved.

Thankfully my new English team Fulham won the First Division with a record 101 points and a ten-point margin over Blackburn Rovers, the runners-up.

I was happy for them, even if I was not so passionate or involved yet, and I felt Fulham was the right choice.

By the end of June I was going back home too but with the pay-per-view TV coming stronger into the market, I knew I could finally watch Fulham's games more often even being in Italy.

By mid-June I eventually received my hard-earned share of the restaurant's service charge, my manager throwing the classic paper bag to my face. A nice touch; I couldn't care less, I was free.

I booked my flight and by the end of the month I was back in Vicenza.

In-Between Years

Soundtrack: 'The Blower's Daughter'
– Damien Rice

NOVEMBER IS the month I was born in and probably it means new beginnings for me as I've often taken big decisions in my life around that date.

In 2002 I started working as a customer operator in the American military base in Vicenza. I had to keep up with my English and that job was a very good option. I was the only male surrounded by seven female colleagues almost hating one another.

We used to work shifts; I was the rookie so the least important in deciding them but being a not-bad-looking 26-year-old I reckon helped a bit in getting along well with all my colleagues.

I was back at playing football so I made a deal with them. I'd take the Saturday night shift, when due, just to get the following Sunday afternoon free to play in the local championship. Done deal, happy boy.

One day at a friend's dinner another mate of mine, who had previously lived for a few years near Gatwick, showed up with an Italian guy he met over there. Giampaolo was one of those people you'd instantly love; a big, tall man with a contagious smile, and mutual sympathy kicked in immediately.

Unfortunately for him he was an Inter Milan fan who also followed Chelsea from time to time – I don't know what's worse to be honest – but besides that we really got on very well.

He was originally from a village in the northern part of my province so we spoke the same dialect, and we kept in touch. Sometime later he said he was a bit tired of living abroad and needed a new challenge. He had good English so I asked my supervisor if she could help. I don't believe much in coincidences, I just reckon that you get to meet who you're looking for, and the base switchboard could do with two more people helping out so shortly after that Giampaolo became my colleague.

Our relationship developed into a great friendship. I helped him find a place to stay in the area my girlfriend was living in and where I was playing football with the local team.

We used to watch a lot of games together and after a short trip to see his girlfriend back in the UK he showed up at my house presenting me with a copy of *FIFA 2004*. 'Now you can play with Fulham,' he laughed.

Only God knows how many hours we spent battling with that video game! I was picking Fulham or Vicenza, sometimes Juventus; he dared to play as Inter and Chelsea. I was the one winning 99 per cent of the games; he was the one scoring a screamer from midfield or the out-of-nowhere odd goal.

After a few months, his partner Rachel decided to join him in Italy and she stayed a bit before they decided to move to New Zealand for a sabbatical year.

I was torn; they wanted me to go but I was working, I had a girlfriend and was captain of my football team so I decided to stay. Yes, you can call me all names you want to.

Fulham did well in their first two seasons back in the Premier League and I managed to watch their games live a few times. I liked Luís Boa Morte and Steed Malbranque and was pissed off when Louis Saha, my favourite player by a mile, was sold to Manchester United. Okay, he deserved a 'bigger club', but I was really annoyed to see him going.

In the summer of 2002 Fulham even won a European competition. We're talking about the old Intertoto Cup, which earned access, if won, to the UEFA Cup. I managed to follow it as games were shown on national channels and not on pay-per-view ones and some Italian teams were included. Fulham beat Finnish and Greek minnows thanks to Steve Marlet's goals. Then they won 3-0 on aggregate against Sochaux, earning access to the final against Bologna, who arrived flying after dismantling FK Teplice 8-2 over two legs. But Fulham, after drawing 2-2 away with Italy star Giuseppe Signori scoring a brace for the home side and Junichi Inamoto and Sylvain Legwinski levelling, won the cup at Loftus Road thanks again to the little Japanese wizard Inamoto, who scored a hat-trick.

They then disposed of two Croatian sides, Hajduk Split (3-2) and Dinamo Zagreb (5-1) before being knocked out by Hertha Berlin 2-1 on aggregate.

Away from football, Paolo and Rachel kept me updated on their new Kiwi life, emailing pictures of their adventures in that amazing land while I became more and more frustrated with my routine. My relationship was perfect from the outside but I was not ready to set up a family yet, and my contract at work was terminated when Germany gathered all switchboards in Europe on their soil, so, being temporary, after almost two years I had to choose between applying for another position or leaving.

I was turning 29 and to be honest not really feeling happy with myself working for a military installation any more. I've never liked wars, guns or weapons and did my military service only because it was compulsory so I thanked everybody for the opportunity and said goodbye.

Not long afterwards I began working for a language school. It was interesting and never boring; my boss was an English lady so I could keep practising.

I was going to Vicenza's games any time I could but after another change of hands and a dismissed manager, who was then recalled after the new one didn't improve the situation, we suffered relegation via the play-off to Serie C, the Italian League 1. It was hell.

Juventus had an incredible squad for the 2004/05 season: Gianluigi Buffon, Emerson, Zlatan Ibrahimović, Alessandro Del Piero, Pavel Nedvěd, Mauro Camoranesi, David Trezeguet, Gianluca Zambrotta, Lilian Thuram, Fabio Cannavaro. A team of stars managed by Fabio Capello easily won the Serie A title but again failed in the Champions League, going out to Liverpool in the quarter-final.

In the Premier League, José Mourinho's Chelsea were the champions while Fulham finished in a safe 13th position, 11 points above relegation. Arsenal's Thierry Henry, sold too soon by Juve, was the top goalscorer with 25.

I was considering my life. I missed London and it was like an unfinished business; those seven months I had spent there were good, the money I saved turned out to be great with the currency exchange rate but in the end I left without knowing the city, never fully enjoying its potential, and never going to a football match.

One never too many.

On top of that, the memory of one morning when I was walking around Queen's Park was still giving me goose bumps.

I lived there for the last couple of months of my stay. and one morning I was walking by, the pavement covered in leaves, I was not thinking about anything in particular when that thought hit me hard. I had to stop; the feeling of having been living in London all my life got me. It was a strange but pleasant feeling that lasted for a few seconds.

I thought about it many times, and then one day, in one of his usual emails, Giampaolo told me they were coming back from New Zealand, and they wanted to move back to England.

'Are you coming with us this time?'

As the Latins used to say, 'To err is human, to persist is diabolical', so the day after, my one-month notice was on my boss's desk and my car, a brand-new Peugeot 307, was up for sale. At the time I was back living with my parents so the sign was off just before getting home.

What's that song about London?

Here to Stay

Soundtrack: 'London Calling' – The Clash

I THINK I told my mum and dad just 48 hours before I left that I was moving again to London, my old man talking to me face to face possibly for the very first time in my life and my mum trying to understand why and asking me why not stay and enjoy the usual weekend abroad here and there.

So, on a Sunday morning of June 2005 with Giampaolo's Volkswagen Golf loaded with all the important stuff – clothes, shoes, local goods including cheese, salami, wine and a PlayStation – we got on the road. We crossed Germany then headed up to Brussels, reaching Calais at the end of our three-day trip.

Just before going to the port we decided to get something to eat, 'I go, I speak a bit of French,' he said. He came back with some ham, a drink and some ready-to-bake bread. Typical Giampaolo.

The White Cliffs of Dover welcomed us back to England. I was feeling optimistic, full of pure happiness.

My dear friend Umberto, again, opened his house for me. I was there living at 112 Topsham Road in Tooting once more after five years.

Through the same agency I had got a job with during my first stay, I found myself working as a barman/waiter at the Barbarella Restaurant on Fulham Road. Right in front of Stamford Bridge. Well, okay, sometimes you have to compromise in life, don't you?

I soon discovered that the Barbarella used to be one of the places to go in the 1970s and 80s thanks to its indoor dancing room located in between the two big dining rooms. Now it was a badly run, old-fashioned place serving below-average-quality food, and supposed to be Italian but with a full Egyptian cooking staff. There were almost no customers on weekdays but it got packed during the weekend with big parties.

We were open only for dinner and closed on Sunday and that was really cool, as it meant a lot of free time and Sunday off.

On my mind only was one thing: to settle down, adjust to London again and go to Craven Cottage to finally attend a Fulham game. Chris 'Cookie' Coleman was still in charge of the Whites and planning for the new season. I couldn't wait; Fulham season tickets were also quite affordable so I was really looking forward to it.

But every Londoner's plans were due to change soon.

One morning, Umberto woke me up almost giving me a heart attack, telling me, 'Call your mum and tell her you're safe, they've just bombed the city!' Well, that's not the words you'd like to be woken up with, and it took me a little to understand what was happening, but footage on Sky News did the job.

Umberto's landline was already off so I reached for the public phone down the road. It was working. My mum begged me in tears to come home and I explained I was fine, safe and sound away from the disaster, then I went back to Umberto's. We watched the news and it was crazy. When you live in a big city like London you can accept that life can be completely different from in a little town as Vicenza but that was really something else.

I still get shivers thinking back at commuters no longer listening to music or reading a book but only focused on checking up each and every newcomer on the train. For the whole month of July it was very weird, with nobody talking and a tense silence all the time.

Thankfully it slowly went back to normality, and working at Barbarella was actually interesting. I could certainly write a book just about those days.

Sunday, 14 August 2005, was eventually the first time I attended a Premier League game, but it was not Fulham; Umberto took me with some friends to Highbury for Arsenal v Newcastle. My soft spot for the Gunners meant I was happy to go, and I also had the chance to see Highbury before they took it down.

I really liked the stadium. It was a piece of history and a really charming ground. The famous Clock End, the Arsenal tube station, the game day; it was all new to me and I totally enjoyed it.

Umberto was soon moving back to Italy after more than a decade managing some of London's finest restaurants so that was a great farewell.

Fulham started the season stuttering with just two wins in ten games, against Everton and Liverpool at home.

Then came some mixed results including a narrow away defeat in the derby with Chelsea but, towards the end of the year, there was some big news – I was finally going to go to a game.

Mirko, my mate back home and one passenger of my car on that crazy parade for Vicenza's Coppa Italia win, was coming to visit with two other friends met on the stands of Vicenza's stadium during my terrace years, Franco and Massimo. We were going to the home match versus Aston Villa.

I was over the moon, not only for that but also because due to work I didn't go home for Christmas, which was a pity because it has always been my favourite family day so having friends coming over during that period really cheered me up.

I will also always thank Piero, my veteran colleague at Barbarella, who invited me to spend Christmas Day at his house with his family.

The night of 28 December 2005 was freaking cold. I remember us getting dressed with the thermometer next to the 0°C marker and moments later a good 10cm of snow was covering up everything.

We were all excited and the walk through a white Bishops Park with the Thames just on the side will stay with me forever. Once inside the ground we spent the first 15 minutes talking about how magic Craven Cottage was – the atmosphere, the music, everything looked like what I had always imagined and dreamed of.

The game was a rollercoaster so there was no time to freeze. It finished 3-3 with Fulham going in front three times.

The team was: Crossley, Leacock, Knight, Bocanegra, Rosenior, Christanval, Legwinski, Boa Morte, Radzinski, McBride, Helguson.

Boa Morte and Helguson impressed me, and McBride too, but that goes without saying.

With cold feet but a warm heart, I had finally been at Craven Cottage and I was hooked. I bought the scarf I still wear these days.

Just before the new year, my Italian boss at Barbarella told me he had great news for me. We were going to open on a Sunday for a private party – Fulham were coming to celebrate Christmas!

I couldn't believe his words and I would be meeting my football heroes; I had to get a shirt so they could sign it for me.

The morning after he told me, I jumped on the tube and went into the centre, got off at Oxford Circus and walked towards Tottenham Court Road as I remembered there were some shops selling sport items. I really liked the red away kit so I bought it.

On that Sunday, I was electric. I even got to work earlier than usual. I was about to meet the whole Fulham team, serving them drinks. I was ready with my brand-new shirt in the bag together with a black marker.

The lady who was helping the owners with some events came by. 'So, Simone, are you excited? I'm told you are a big fan of them.'

'Ohh yes, I'm ecstatic, I love Fulham, I even bought the kit for the occasion!'

'You mean Brentford?'

'Brentford?' I was confused

'Yes, Brentford are coming to celebrate tonight.'

WTF, how can you mistake Fulham for bloody Brentford?!

I almost fainted. Those idiots couldn't even distinguish a Premier League club owned by Mr Harrods, Mohamed Al-Fayed, from a team struggling in League One, but, on top of that, one of our historic rivals!

It was Brentford indeed, I couldn't wait for them to leave. I was so pissed off. I was upset and I took it as the final sign that I had to leave Barbarella.

The 2006 Streak

Soundtrack: 'Lucky Man' – The Verve

THE YEAR 2006 started with me looking for a job, tired of working at night and most of all when everybody else was having fun. I wanted to go back to a nine-to-five and after a lucky interview I got employed by a company selling rights-free images. Funnily enough, the office was again in Fulham Road, this time on the right side of Fulham Broadway tube station, and not just geographically.

At the beginning I was also still going to Barbarella during weekends to get some extra money as my salary at the office was not so great.

At Ingram Publishing I was in charge of the mail office, sending out worldwide all the products sold by the sales department. My colleagues were literally from everywhere; Ireland, Italy, Belgium, Scotland, England, Puerto Rico, Spain and Pakistan. I loved that melting pot of cultures.

Fulham had started the year winning four home games in a row, smashing West Bromwich Albion 6-1 and beating Tottenham in one of the numerous London derbies. Form then slumped with four straight defeats as away from Craven Cottage they looked a totally different team and conceded 14 goals, merely scoring three. Renaissance was around the corner though with a 1-0 home win against Chelsea on 19

March thanks to a Boa Morte goal. The routine was inverted in the following two games, drawing away to Villa and getting beaten 3-1 at home by Portsmouth on 1 April. Thankfully it turned out to be a proper April Fool's Day as home duty was promptly resumed at the expense of another London team, Charlton, and then Wigan, ending the month with a nice win on the road as the light-blue half of Manchester turned clear white for one day.

Another season ended with Fulham finishing in a relatively quiet 12th place and the young Dutch talent Collins John as the team's top scorer with 11.

With Premier League status confirmed, fans could start focusing on the forthcoming World Cup in Germany.

I began to sense that 2006 could be a good year when I got the office job, and Fulham staying up was another sign but, great for me, it was just the beginning.

At work I was using TNT a lot as a courier and there was a raffle using some shipment codes where you could win your nation's World Cup kit. I tried and one day I got it, winning Italy's kit. Happy days and I took it as a further sign for good things to come.

The tournament kicked off and for the group stage games I was joining Giampaolo at his mate's house down in West Sussex. Gianni was another Italian but also a Chelsea supporter.

In the group stage, Italy beat Ghana 2-0, with future Fulham favourite John Paintsil in the Africans' starting XI, then drew 1-1 with a US side containing a clear Fulham DNA. Kasey Keller was in goal, Carlos Bocanegra was at centre-back, Brian McBride was in attack – his nose elbowed by Daniele De Rossi – and a certain Clint Dempsey played on the right, the only American to score a goal at the tournament.

Australia awaited in the round of 16 so for the afternoon game, I put my shirt on and thanks to my boss Antonio I got to the pub next door to watch it during a long lunch break, just to realise, once in, that the pub was an Aussie enclave. There were four pubs close to the office and that one was the only one I had never been in before.

I was there, I couldn't retreat, and while ordering my beer a guy not wearing any kit came by. 'I'm Italian too!' he told me.

Well, I was a little relieved, even if in a battle two lightweight Italians would have been quickly disposed of by just the four Australian giants downing XXX beer standing by the wall. Probably even only two of them would have been enough.

When Italy got 'that' penalty, the other Italian started bouncing here and there like a flipper ball. With the four giants ready to hit, I pulled him back to his chair giving him a death stare which eventually tuned him down.

'If we score, you stay quiet or I'll help them beat you up,' was my sweet, encouraging comment to him.

Francesco Totti put it past Mark Schwarzer, another White-to-be, the referee blew the whistle, and the four Aussies put their glasses down while I threw the guy out and quickly followed him before they realised we were gone.

I was happy that Italy avenged that lacklustre display with a cool 3-0 victory over Ukraine in Hamburg four days later in the quarter-final, and it was back to Gianni's for the semi-final against the hosts.

Italy were again in the World Cup Final, 12 years after that heartbreaking skied penalty by my fellow citizen Roberto Baggio in Pasadena.

This occasion called for a bigger venue so together with some English friends, all supporting Italy, we went to Pino's restaurant Portofino in East Grinstead. It goes without saying that it went bananas at the outcome. All of us were celebrating on the roof of the place, firing fireworks and drinking heavily; please don't tell anybody!

I was sorry to see my former favourite Louis Saha on the losing end for France, but not that much.

I wore my shirt on Monday at work and proudly walked around London that day.

While I had never been to that pub, there was instead another one, the Elk, where with my colleagues we were locals.

It was not the typical pub I loved but more like a club where you could have a drink and dance. One night, I pulled one of the bar ladies thanks to Jet's song 'Are You Gonna Be My Girl'. She was a stunning French girl from Brittany. On the way to my place she saw the Italian flag hanging from the window and said, 'Don't tell me that's your place.' Yes, baby. Italy 2 France 0.

Half a year and a World Cup in the bag, with work going well, I loved London even more.

Fulham were preparing for the coming season having already signed Jimmy Bullard from Wigan in May and drawing 0-0 with Real Madrid in a friendly.

On the club's website you could enter a competition to win two tickets for the opening home game. I said to myself, 'Why not?' I applied and, guess what, I won.

After getting thrashed 5-1 at Manchester United, with Saha netting the first goal, Fulham were then kicking off their home 2006/07 campaign against Big Sam Allardyce's Bolton Wanderers, one of those teams I've never liked.

That so-called direct football to me only translates to few ideas stuck in the past. Football is a game in which there's a physical side, of course, but most of all, there should be technique, vision, skills, class. Big Sam's teams have often looked to me like a bunch of giants throwing long balls here and there and then fighting for them.

On Wednesday 23 August, me and Giampaolo enjoyed a stadium tour and then watched the game from the directors' area. Sadly it was a very poor display of football, ending 1-1 thanks to two penalties, Fulham's coming in the 90th minute and scored by new idol Bullard. Well, at least the complimentary cakes at half-time were delicious.

The Whites then returned two wins, including a fine 2-1 away scalp of Newcastle where late McBride and Bocanegra goals overturned Scott Parker's initial home advantage, and a draw before losing the home derby to Chelsea 2-0. Then they drew two away games and beat Charlton in between.

A great fighting spirit saw Fulham quickly forgetting Frank Lampard's double and coming back from two goals down at Watford to almost snatch a win, then they drew at Aston Villa after being one down.

So when Wigan left the Cottage with all three points and Fulham didn't manage to score a single goal, I reckon many fans were confused to say the least.

During that autumn some friends of Giampaolo came to visit him from his home town in Italy and I got to meet the girl who in winter became my new girlfriend in a long-distance relationship. Elisabetta was a very beautiful ballerina.

Before that, though, my lucky streak continued when, while withdrawing money from a cash machine, I saw you could enter another football-related competition which at first I didn't understand properly but as usual, I decided to give it a go.

Every time you withdrew money you received a ticket with a code you had to enter into the dedicated website, choosing the Premier League team you supported. There would have been one winner per week, and 11 weeks for each club.

Days went by trying my luck and I almost forgot about it until this:

I couldn't believe it! I was super happy when I received my very own Fulham shirt with my surname on the back together with the number seven, which was the week number I won in. Funnily enough, the number seven was the first number I wore when I started playing football.

I must admit that the night I got it I slept with it on.

My great friend Umberto decided to move back to Italy to be closer to his daughter Alice, so he sold the house and I had to move. After looking at some new areas closer to work I instead found a great room in Balham, in a nice Victorian House where I'd be sharing a roof with two English guys, a French girl, an English girl and Mr Cook, a Scottish gentleman, who was the owner.

They asked me if I supported any football team. I replied I was a Fulham fan and they were quite surprised. Their first question was, 'Why Fulham?'

I laughed.

In the end it went well and I was moving in. The English men were Scunthorpe and Liverpool fans respectively while Mr Cook was Chelsea. Well, it can't go always right, can it?

That detail was soon forgotten as Fulham gave me a nice birthday present by beating Everton 1-0 at home, in an up-and-down month of November, and stunning Arsenal 2-1 at the Cottage.

The Day I Almost Signed
for Fulham

Soundtrack: 'Lose Yourself' – Eminem

THE NEW place was cool. It needed a few improvements here and there but I was feeling sufficiently at home; the living room was fully equipped with Sky Sports too and that was definitely a plus.

I got on well with everybody from the beginning and during the weekend there was always a game on to watch with Mr Cook who, despite supporting the wrong team in Fulham, turned out being a really nice and helping figure.

He told me he started following Chelsea in his early days in London due to the presence of a namesake Cook in their ranks. He was not one of the new breed of plastic supporters who became Chelsea fans after Roman Abramovich's millions made the club punch at the same level of the world's usual heavyweights, so he deserved my respect.

I really liked Balham. It was very well connected to almost everywhere, being served by both the tube and overground services, and I just needed the train to reach West Brompton station then I had a 15-minute walk to the office. There were plenty of restaurants, bars, shops and even a very good Italian pizzeria with very reasonable prices.

The street we were living in was also very quiet with nearly no cars passing by the whole day, and I could go for a run to the common just round the corner.

Between the end of 2006 and the beginning of 2007, Fulham drew an incredible six games in a row, including a good 2-2 at Stamford Bridge and a 1-1 at home to Spurs thanks to Vincenzo Montella, my countryman just signed on loan from AS Roma.

One day at work I was going through the mail when I bumped into a Fulham-marked letter addressed to me.

And even if they called me Ms Simone, the reality was getting closer: I'd walk on the pitch of my beloved Craven Cottage in a Fulham shirt with the chance of even getting a Fulham contract. Please don't wake me up!

So here I am, on Wednesday, 3 February 2007, walking into the ground in Fulham colours holding a football with my number seven together with ten strangers also wearing a kit and carrying a football, posing as a team and being taken pictures of. Really?!

Days before, we were asked who our favourite Fulham player was at the time. I answered Boa Morte, who joined West Ham quickly after and people didn't take it well so when the announcer introduced us a little and reported that I got booed. Jeez, I haven't kicked a ball yet and you already boo me!

Well, here we are, ten males, one female next to me wearing number six, surname Coleman. Somebody comes to us, places our footballs in a box and clumsily mixes them. He then bends himself into the box, coming out holding one football which has another one on top. That one falls back into the box – it's the number seven, the winner is number six, Miss Coleman, who blushes and doesn't speak or celebrate.

My dreams of being the winner crash like thin glass and my idea of celebrating like Montella's aeroplane move around the pitch gets busted. Everybody moves away with our 15 minutes of Warhol-esque fame gone, heading back to reality, while Miss Coleman will receive the £10,000 signing-on fee, a squad number, a photo with the first team, the chance to train with them, and a signed shirt.

Okay, you can shoot me now.

Not in the best mood of my life, I watch the game which at last saw us pick up a win, 2-1 over Newcastle with goals from Helguson and McBride. Why I didn't say Helguson was my favourite player, I still don't know.

Unfortunately that would be Fulham's last win for a long time, also losing 2-1 against Bolton and Manchester United in their last two Premier League games of the month. A bizarre March would instead see the Whites draw all their three games to not-so-unbeatable opposition in Villa, Wigan and Portsmouth, two of those matches being played at home.

A change in pace was badly needed but unfortunately it came the other way round, Everton getting their home revenge with a 4-1 win and Manchester City running away from Stevenage Road 3-1 victors. This game unfortunately cost 'Cookie' Coleman his job and he was replaced by Lawrie Sanchez, who was doing well managing Northern Ireland.

Things got worse and many were questioning Al-Fayed's decision to sack Coleman. Fulham came away empty-handed from Reading before drawing at home to Blackburn and being again on the receiving end of a revenge beating, this time by Arsenal, who defeated us with two late goals at the Emirates Stadium, their new ground.

Thankfully, Fulham had eventually signed that bright US talent Clint Dempsey; he was thrown in the den of the vital home game versus Liverpool and responded by scoring the only goal of the match, which saw Fulham guaranteed safety.

So 5 May was again a lucky date – Inter Milan's away defeat in 2002 gifted Juventus the title, and now this.

The 2007/08 seaason will see again Fulham playing in the Premier League, YES!

The Great Escape

Soundtrack: 'The Great Escape' –
Elmer Bernstein

I HONESTLY still have no clue why I didn't get a season ticket to Fulham those years. I had the money, I liked Fulham a lot, and there's no explanation whatsoever.

Anyway, 2007 was past its mid-point, at work we were selling more online subscriptions than physical products and I moved into sales, which meant more money, and more fun.

My long-distance relationship was going well and Elisabetta eventually even moved to London for the summer.

At 32 I felt I could still play some football somewhere so I started looking for a team and found one in Chiswick. It didn't go as well as it promised to at the beginning but at least something nice happened.

One day we were playing in a park somewhere in the middle of nowhere, but still in west London. Changing rooms didn't exist but it didn't matter, I liked that style. We had lost the game, and almost everybody left as it was really cold and we were wet and covered in mud. I went to get my tracksuit jacket and running back to the parking lot I saw something was left on the grass. It was a 2005/06 Fulham home shirt. I looked for the opponents as there were no Fulham supporters in my team, but literally everybody was gone.

Well, if someone had to find that it had to be me, so it was now in good hands.

Remaining with Fulham, having 'saved' us, Lawrie Sanchez was rewarded with a three-year contract. The squad was then revolutionised with a massive 15 new faces in and eight players leaving including icons such as 'my' Heiðr Helguson and 'The Wardrobe' Papa Bouba Diop. Liam Rosenior and Michael Brown, who even captained the side, were also among those saying goodbye.

Between all the new signings, I was surprised somebody of the calibre of Danny Murphy accepted to come to a side which barely stayed up the year before and surely didn't aim for much more than repeating that feat.

Al-Fayed, probably worried by the events, went back splashing the cash: £4m spent on Steven Davis from Villa and £6m for Diomansy Kamara from West Bromwich Albion with only two free signings and two loans. Eight new players were also from the UK.

Even if I didn't like Sanchez's old-school style of play I was optimistic. Aaron Hughes, Paul Konchesky and Dejan Stefanović all had good pedigrees. A further £6m was spent on Chris Baird from Southampton and the Algerian winger Hameur Bouazza from Watford. Lee Cook, an exciting prospect who made the short trip from Queens Park Rangers, was signed for £2.5m. South Korean international Ki joined from Reading.

Sanchez then wanted his fellow countryman David Healy and signed the experienced goalkeeper Kasey Keller from Borussia Mönchengladbach; almost all new signings had Premier League experience.

A quiet mid-table season looked likely but it didn't start like that. Fulham's first ten games were awful and featured a solitary win, 2-1 at home to Bolton with Helguson scoring at the Cottage but in opposition colours.

Six draws in seven games included two 3-3 home rollercoasters with Tottenham – Kamara's bicycle kick earning us a point in the 90th minute – and Manchester City, after being ahead twice with Bouazza scoring a fierce free kick.

A goalless draw away to Chelsea was in that sequence, and by the end of October there had also been four defeats – three of them by the same 2-1 scoreline.

The first had come against Arsenal on the opening day after Healy had put us in front in the first minute just for Robin van Persie to level with an 84th-minute penalty and Aleksandr Hleb to seal it for the Gunners with the last kick of the match. That was a worrying sign of things to come.

Getting in front and ending up beaten or with just a point became a very dangerous habit and continued at home to Middlesbrough, away to Villa, away to Wigan, at home to City and away to Sunderland.

For the home game versus Derby County I tried to bring good luck but it only partly worked and a poor 0-0 draw was the final result.

Eventually, probably knowing about my birthday on 1 November, Fulham were back to winning ways three days later, 3-1 at home to Reading. But again that remained the sole victory of the month.

The Whites were well beaten 2-0 at Liverpool and drew 2-2 at home to Blackburn after again being two times in front.

But if November was bad, December was even worse. Three defeats in a row without scoring a goal, a poor 1-1 home draw with Wigan after being a goal down, and then a devastating 5-1 smashing away to Spurs ruined the Christmas period.

On 28 December, the well-travelled former Blackburn Rovers and Inter Milan manager Roy Hodgson was appointed as Fulham's new head coach. His CV spoke for itself, even if Roberto Carlos stated that he left Inter for Real Madrid due to Hodgson playing him more advanced than his preferred left-back position. The Croydon-born manager had previously won the Swedish league, twice with Halmstads and twice with Malmö; he also took Switzerland to the 1994 World Cup almost unbeaten and qualified for the 1996 European Championship in England. He then won a title in Denmark and had also been linked to the national-team positions with Germany and England in previous years.

I personally didn't know what to think. I remembered Hodgson in Italy both at Inter and Udinese, and I simply thought it could not be worse than Sanchez.

The first game of the new era didn't look like anything new, Fulham losing 2-1 in the home derby to their bitter blue enemies after again being one up. Then they lost 2-1 against another London side, this time West Ham, once more after being in front. Then came Arsenal walking away from the Cottage with a 3-0 victory.

Following that, 2008 started with three defeats in three. Worrying times for sure. It didn't look like the change of manager was going to work and many friends were taking the piss but hey, that's what you get when you don't support superpowers, so yes I was sad but it was my decision to support Fulham and I was definitely not going to change it. Faith is faith in good and bad times.

January at least meant the transfer market was open and Hodgson pulled the strings of his contacts in the north. Brede Hangeland, a Norwegian giant, was signed from Copenhagen. Leon Andreasen, a Danish international, came from Werder Bremen, Toni Kallio and Jari Litmanen, two Finland internationals albeit a bit past their best, also came in.

Litmanen was a player I used to admire at Ajax as a really clever and classy number ten who faced Juventus in the Champions League Final the last time the Bianconeri won it.

A 0-0 draw away to Bolton to end January and a much-needed 2-1 home win over Villa, after Hughes's own goal seemed to all but condemn Fulham to relegation, were a breath of fresh air that unfortunately lasted for just one week as my beloved Cottagers lost another three games in a row and without scoring a single goal.

I had already started my mission of making Fulham popular back home in Italy. I was telling all my friends and former team-mates about my passion for them but results weren't helping.

When my sister took my younger nephew with her to come and see me, besides being very happy, I took it as a chance to get him on board as a new Fulham fan.

So, all proudly wearing the colours, we attended the home game against West Ham on 23 February 2008.

Unfortunately Nolberto Solano broke our hearts after Antti Niemi was clearly fouled. All signs were against Fulham. Usually, when you're poor, it seems that also referees' decisions and luck go against you.

We then had to thank Jimmy Bullard again for rescuing a point in the 89th minute at Blackburn. The table didn't lie; our situation was critical, especially because the morale didn't look great either. No surprise.

During those years, however, home games against Everton had often been productive and it was once again the case this time around thanks to Brian McBride's second-half header.

But it was only Fulham's fourth win of the season so far and they were four points from safety by mid-March.

Again it was a short-lived smile for all of us as Fulham lost 2-0 at Newcastle then drew 2-2 away to Derby, being 2-1 up with 12 minutes to go, before losing again at home, 3-1 to Sunderland. Craven Cottage, our usual fortress, was now just an easy, open-door castle with free entrance.

There were some sparks of life again on the road with a vital win 2-0 at Reading when our new striker, Erik Nevland, bagged the final goal after a few good saves by their goalkeeper and us hitting the goal frame too many times. Reading, just above us, were the only team we could try to reach for safety.

Liverpool then left Craven Cottage with all three points as bookies and newspapers were all sure of our fate; probably even the most die-hard Fulham fan had little hope left too. With three games to go we needed three wins and a lot of, possibly too much, luck.

On Saturday, 26 April 2008, I was home, tired after a long week of work and gym training. I lay on the sofa, the house almost empty or just very quiet, with somebody definitely recovering from a Friday night out and so with a hangover to nurse. I had lunch on my own and felt a little melancholic.

Manchester City v Fulham was live, so I was watching. In the tenth minute Stephen Ireland put City 1-0 up, then in the 21st Benjami made it 2-0. We were all but relegated. I remember some tears; I punched the sofa and, yes, I admit, cursed God in a proper Italian way. Then I fell asleep.

I woke up; the TV was still on so with a barely opened eye I checked the score. It was 2-1 as Kamara had scored in the 70th minute. I sat, holding my fists. When you believe in something or somebody and things don't go right, sadness can take control but just the thinner ray of light can propel real trust to come out again. That's what happened here.

Fulham were now pressing high and won a penalty. Murphy took it. Saved. Shit. But he scored for 2-2 and I screamed loudly. Very loudly.

Reading were still 0-0 away to Wigan and in the 90th minute Fulham were again attacking in numbers. A great through ball by Murphy saw Kamara run and blast his shot beyond Joe Hart. I turned crazy, jumping around the living room screaming with joy. Mr Cook came down, briefly looked at the TV, and started applauding. I ran and hugged him, improvising a silly dance.

The result gave Fulham a chance with our next game at home to Birmingham, while Reading would be hosting Tottenham. I had to go so I jumped to the stairs and into my room, grabbed my laptop, checked Fulham's website and got a ticket in the Putney End.

It's 3 May 2008, Craven Cottage is packed, and the Putney End is full with a good presence of Bluenoses who are making some noise. The game is nervous as there's a lot at stake.

Fulham start again with Keller in goal, Bullard partners Murphy in the middle with Davies and Dempsey on the flanks, Kamara and McBride are up front. Former Whites favourite Maik Taylor is in goal for Birmingham.

The first half is goalless, I'm concerned, and there's an idiot, a Brum supporter, who is making me even more nervous going around the Putney End screaming at us, spitting here and there, menacing and really annoying quite a few people. Stewards are too nice and naïve and he keeps on taking the piss, clearly drunk and possibly high on something. Hey, he's free to do that, mind you, as far as you 'don't break my balls' as we say back home.

In the 52nd minute, Bullard puts a free kick into the box, McBride arrives and scores with his head, and pandemonium erupts. YES!

That idiot comes again at us, his arms wide open, confronting people randomly. He comes near me, I get up, spread my arms and shout 'YESSSSSSSSS', but he spits near me. Couldn't even get me, cu*t! Yes, bad words are still the very first you learn in a foreign language.

Birmingham are not threatening Keller and Fulham are in control but we need the second goal, as you never know in football.

In the 87th minute, Nevland wins the ball and runs towards Taylor. Everybody is standing up, come on, shoot, shoot for fuck's sake! A defender comes close, Nevland shoots and it's 2-0. COME ON!

I find myself together with another dozen of us confronting the shaved tosser spreading insults all red-faced and almost having a heart attack; stewards this time react and block him, delivering him back to his mates.

Fulham 2 Birmingham 0, Reading 0 Tottenham 1, Craven Cottage is getting mental and now our future is in our hands.

I have to go to Portsmouth for the last game of the year, I must go.

No, shit, wait a minute. I realise I've got my flight booked to go home as one of my best mates is getting married. Jeez, why so early? Stay together, postpone the wedding; I want to go and see Fulham. My full love for Fulham has to take a little break, unfortunately I can't go to Pompey away, but I make a promise with Mr Cook because when you make a promise with a witness, you're always more committed on keeping it.

If we stay up I'll become a season ticket holder. Deal.

The wedding is nice, I'm seeing people I haven't seen for ages, the day is also pleasant with a lovely sun, and I keep checking the phone waiting for Mr Cook's updates. He says we're playing well but it's still 0-0. Food is great as is the wine, and I need some alcohol as the tension is killing me.

There are just 15 minutes to go and we are still drawing while Reading are thumping a derelict Derby side 3-0 away. If it ends like this we're down. Come on boys, we can't go down after all the fighting and the renewed hope.

My phone vibrates. It's a goal, it's Murphy, it's 1-0 to Fulham!

The match ends, Fulham stay up, and I'm jumping around all dressed up waving my tie in the air and singing 'we're stayin' up and we're stayin' up!' The other guests laugh as I try to explain but nearly nobody knows Fulham. I don't care. We have survived, the Great Escape is complete and I need to sit down before an ambulance is required.

Seventh Heaven

Soundtrack: 'Your Hand in Mine'
– Explosions in the Sky

ONCE BACK from Italy, I celebrated with my house-mates. Phil the Scunthorpe fan told me he'd come to the Cottage anytime, Mr Cook, still a Chelsea supporter let's not forget, was already visiting the best ground in the world as his mate had two season tickets and from time to time he was invited to clear his soul by the Thames. Wendy also told me she wanted to come and watch Fulham sooner or later. I was spreading the faith.

More and more friends were developing sympathy for the Whites while my nephews were already hooked and checking out Fulham scores on a regular basis, also watching all live games on Sky.

During the transfer market the squad was once again revamped and our dear president didn't keep his wallet closed. Andy Johnson arrived from Everton for £12.5m, then we paid West Ham over £6m to pocket Bobby Zamora and John Paintsil. Fredrik Stoor and Dickson Etuhu also joined in from Rosenborg and Sunderland respectively. The best pieces of business turned out to be the captures of Mark Schwarzer from Middlesbrough and Zoltán Gera from West Brom, both free agents, and the one of the unknown Chris Smalling from minnows Maidstone United for the equivalent of pocket money. Toni Kallio was rewarded with a full contract while Pascal Zuberbühler, an experienced and travelled goalkeeper, came in for free.

Some sad eyes were seen around Stevenage Road for the departure of captain Brian McBride, going back home to play for Chicago in the MLS, while Carlos Bocanegra joined Rennes in France. The Northern Ireland brigade also lost three components: David Healy was sold to Sunderland, Steven Davis to Rangers, and Michael Timlin to Swindon Town on a free. Paul Stalteri, who had enjoyed a good spell, went back to parent club Tottenham and veterans Philippe Christanval and Ian Pearce also left. In total, 13 players signed and 19 left.

There was a renovated enthusiasm around Fulham. The thrilling way we survived gave everybody a rush of adrenaline which wasn't going to disappear so quickly. To me, it was much better than a quiet mid-table finish.

My first season ticket card had already come in the post and I was super excited. I went to Sardinia on holiday in August, needing some sun and vitamin D. I came back just in time for the beginning of the Premier League season. Who would expect though that the opening game was like going back to a nightmare, a 2-1 loss away to newly promoted Hull City after being one up?

I was astonished. Hey, we know every game is hard in the top flight, but all our reborn confidence and dreams were both shattered with the very first kicks of the new season.

That was when I got more used to the word Fulhamish – when you're up and you then get beaten, or you get a good result against big teams like Manchester United or Liverpool just to lose to Wigan or Bolton the following game, that's Fulhamish.

So when Arsenal came to the Cottage for the start of the home campaign, we were worried. But no, Brede Hangeland's goal was enough to win the game and restore our happiness. Isn't it Fulhamish?

For our next Premier League game we all had to wait until mid-September and the 'usual' 2-1 win at home to Bolton. Gera and Zamora were already showing why their signings were coups.

But we were back in limbo when Fulham suffered three defeats in a row – losing at Blackburn and West Brom away while West Ham left the Cottage successful.

Two draws then followed, 0-0 at home to Sunderland and 1-1 away to our lucky harbour in Portsmouth, with two points in five games bringing back unnecessary old fears.

The team needed time to gel but getting just five points from games with Hull, Bolton, Blackburn, West Brom, Sunderland and Pompey didn't look like a change in fortune from the previous two seasons.

Hodgson's preferred starting XI seemed to be this:

Schwarzer
Paintsil; Hughes; Hangeland; Konchesky
Davies; Bullard; Murphy; Gera
Johnson; Zamora

Loyal to his classic 4-4-2 scheme though, our manager's tactics rose more than an eyebrow as a newer philosophy of football was impacting the world and supporters, me included, would have loved a more fluent and attacking way of playing the most beautiful game on earth.

I must admit that our next match, Wigan at home, worried me more than United or Chelsea. Thankfully Andy Johnson decided to start showing why he was worth £12.5m and his brace was more than enough to give us some tranquillity.

My birthday this time was without a gift from Fulham as we lost 1-0 to Everton at Goodison Park and fell back into muddy waters.

At least the Cottage became our safe house again and Newcastle were dispatched with our beloved signature, 2-1. Johnson scored and Murphy resumed his penalty-taker duties with success.

And the same scoreline was stamped on Spurs the following week, Johnson confirming his presence on the score sheet.

Three wins in four games got the season back on track and Hodgson was smiling with a visit to Liverpool looming next. A crucial game; would we be back to sweating times or keeping up with our new status of a club on the rise with promising performances?

The resulting 0-0 draw said a lot. Fulham had become a team nobody would like to face – not spectacular but solid, not scoring a lot but also not conceding a lot.

For me, this was the real turning point and another confirmation, if needed, followed at Villa Park with another 0-0 draw. Consistency in results had almost been forgotten for Fulham.

The run of draws soon reached four in a row with a 1-1 at home to Manchester City being followed by a 0-0 at Stoke.

On 20 December we smashed Middlesbrough 3-0 at home then on Boxing Day we again came back from a difficult away game without conceding, drawing 0-0 at White Hart Lane. Next to come would be Chelsea at home.

I was in Italy on holiday; living abroad made me desire Christmas even more. After celebrating with the family I travelled to Turin to see some old friends and Juventus lovers. Before accepting the invitation I made one thing clear, 'I'll come if you let me watch the Fulham game.' Deal. So I found myself and my friend Fabio sat on the sofa. I warned his wife

Stella that I would scream if we scored, and she was fine with that. She was used to her hubby doing the same week-in week-out with Juventus.

And it didn't take long for me to do so as Dempsey, for whom I had started having a great admiration, put us in front after just ten minutes. The first half ended with Fulham 1-0 – this was how Christmas should be.

The second half brought me back down to earth though as Frank Lampard bagged a brace mostly thanks to an unusually shaky Schwarzer. All signs were that we would lose to our bitter rivals who could count on names like Didier Drogba, Deco and Nicolas Anelka in their ranks.

My friend tried to cheer me up. I was grumpy, couldn't be quiet, downed my beer quickly and kept shaking my legs. In the 89th minute we got a corner. It was a good ball in, Demps rose again with a good header, and YES! My friend was celebrating too, laughing at me and my craziness. The Hammersmith End looked like a boiling pot, brilliant! Stella came into the living room, finding her hubby and me jumping around drinking beer. She sighed and left.

It was a great way to dispatch 2008 and I couldn't have been happier. I flew back to London with my batteries recharged, my heart pampered by family and friends and a team, Fulham, for which my passion was constantly growing.

The new year started well at work where I was getting more and more comfortable. Sales were high so I could enjoy an expensive city like London without worrying too much. Concerts, restaurants, little trips here and there; good times.

The away game to West Ham was our first of 2009 in the Premier League so I decided to go. Upton Park was a stadium I liked a lot; it had charisma, history, and a visit was a must.

On the way there I remembered when back at the beginning of 2001 me and my mates went to have a look at a flat in Plaistow. With all due respect, it was not London's most sought-after borough. Things hadn't changed much and the neighbourhood was still a bit rough. It reminded me of difficult areas usually portrayed in those gritty British movies I like a lot, such as those by Shane Meadows: *Somers Town*, *This Is England* and *A Room for Romeo Brass* the first that come to mind.

Upton Park was like it always seemed on TV, amazing with its two towers by the main gate. West Ham's supporters have always been famously loud and so it was here with 'I'm Forever Blowing Bubbles' being sung loudly and also helping make the trip worthwhile.

Some naughty bubble was still floating though when my countryman David Di Michele put West Ham in front.

Fulham looked lively and Paul Konchesky received the ball on the left then charged forward, passing the midfield line and keeping going before firing a thunderbolt out of nowhere straight into the top corner. What a strike!

The tradition of a former West Ham player scoring against his old team was respected and the match was level, so it was hard to take when in the second half Mark Noble and Carlton Cole won it for the hosts.

Our great streak had been broken and we suffered as a result as we came back empty-handed from the following trip to Sunderland.

But it was quite clear we were not the old, shy, frightened Fulham and the boys highlighted that at home to Portsmouth, convincingly winning 3-1 thanks to Johnson as usual and a double by Erik Nevland.

A point away to Wigan followed that before getting well beaten 3-0 at Manchester United, although that defeat was promptly recovered a few days later at Craven Cottage when West Brom were punished by Zamora and a punctual Johnson.

A very positive season that everybody needed continued as Fulham travelled to the Emirates and came back with a point without conceding to an attack led by Robin van Persie.

Fulhamish enough, we then allowed Hull City to complete the double against us, losing 1-0 in the 93rd minute, and even more so when Blackburn beat us 2-1 despite Dempsey putting us in front just after two minutes.

But as a constant feat during this epic season, Fulham, like the phoenix, rose again and conquered Bolton 3-1.

Just over a month after our visit to Old Trafford, we welcomed the league leaders, the Red Devils boasting Cristiano Ronaldo, Dimitar Berbatov, Ryan Giggs, Wayne Rooney, Paul Scholes and Patrice Evra among others.

But after just 18 minutes the ginger superstar Scholes turned keeper to save Zamora's header, was sent off, and Murphy put us 1-0 up with the penalty. But United have never been a team afraid to play with one man down so the game was far from finished. Thankfully Schwarzer was at his best on a few occasions and before also Rooney saw red, Gera scored and a famous win was recorded.

These are the home games you like to be at – giantkilling afternoons that give your ego a nice pat.

The following home defeat to Liverpool was a photocopy of the Hull game where we again conceded in the dying minutes to go down 1-0.

But in a crazy season we came away from the other half of Manchester with a resounding 3-1 win with Dempsey bagging a brace.

We returned from the north-east with a 0-0 draw at Middlesbrough before Nevland's goal was enough for another three points at the Cottage in the 1-0 defeat of Stoke.

The 3-1 loss in the derby with Chelsea was painful only for us fans because the boys cancelled it out with two comfortable wins in a row, 3-1 at home over Villa and a 1-0 steal in Newcastle mostly thanks to Kamara's three goals in two games.

It was a great pity when we lost the last game of this glorious season, 2-0 to Everton at home, but we finished seventh with an incredible 53 points, our highest finish ever in the top flight.

The icing on the cake was qualification for the Europa League, as the UEFA Cup had been renamed.

Only a year previously we were at the end of the season and praying for a win at Portsmouth to stay up after an awful campaign which saw us almost condemned to the Championship; now we were looking at a European tour.

Could there be anything more Fulhamish than that?

My Ground, My Seat, My Fulham

Soundtrack: 'Come With Me' –
Puff Daddy feat. Jimmy Page

IT'S MY fourth year in London and things are going well. Work is fine and I'm training regularly at the gym in Clapham Junction after it. My girlfriend is gone but the city is full of opportunities in that field so no need to worry.

When you're an immigrant, relationships are possibly even more important. I've always valued true friendships very highly and I'm happy I've quite a few strong ones over here already. Besides Giampaolo, Mr Cook has become a very important figure in my life; he's 30 years older than me so he could easily be my dad.

Quite frequently we spend the Sunday together cooking and then watching football. We talk a lot and he's a very wise person I like to listen to.

I'm still buzzing from the 2008/09 exploits and it's already time for the new season. The best work in the transfer market is to keep hold of our top players and in doing so Al-Fayed and all the staff really did a great job. Hangeland, Murphy, Zamora, Dempsey, Gera all stayed. And if last year's magic looked amazing, I believe that signing Damien Duff was really producing a rabbit from the hat.

A talented, experienced left-footed midfielder with also plenty of international football in his legs whose purchase makes you understand how Fulham's reputation has grown fast. Irishman Stephen Kelly and Englishman Jonathan Greening arrive from the city of Birmingham, the latter from West Brom. South African international Kagisho Dikgacoi is instead the exotic addition.

Goodbyes are again sad as the beloved Moritz Volz is released together with former starlet Collins John. They are joined by quite a few other faces including Bouazza and Ki. Leon Andreasen, after a few good games with us, joins Hannover permanently.

After an easy summer tour of Australia the Europa League campaign kicks off with a trip to Lithuania where the literally unknown FK Vétra awaits. A 6-0 aggregate win boosts our enthusiasm and sees us reach the play-off round where the former USSR territory is again our destination, Russian team FC Amkar Perm, who we edge past 3-2 with Zamora and Johnson scoring again.

Fulham are now in the group stage together with CSKA Sofia, Basel and Italian giants AS Roma.

The first six Premier League fixtures see us back to our rollercoaster times. The Whites open the season winning 1-0 at Portsmouth before losing 2-0 to Chelsea at home and then at Aston Villa by the same score. Our faithful 2-1 home win comes back into action at the expense of Everton, but is unfortunately followed by two more defeats to Wolves and Arsenal.

September, definitely a month to forget, is completed by a 1-1 draw away in Sofia but October instead proves to be a month to remember as we ended it unbeaten.

In the Europa League, we start the month with a 1-0 win over Basel and finish with a 1-1 draw at home with Roma in a game we deserved to win but which was full of controversy. Two wins and two draws come in the Premier League. The draws are both 2-2, at West Ham and Manchester City, while Hull are beaten 2-0 and Liverpool are given a 3-1 thumping to restore confidence. In the only Europa League game of November, the trip to Rome – *caput mundi*, the capital of the world – ended in a harsh 2-1 defeat as Fulham finished with with nine men.

With the Whites in a more comfortable position in the table, the away defeat at Birmingham is easily digested being surrounded by two 1-1 away draws to Wigan and Bolton, both from being a goal down. There is a good, emphatic 3-0 demolition of Blackburn on home soil with Dempsey, whose importance in the squad keeps growing, bagging a brace.

December is already here and it's a real pity that we close it with a defeat during the typical Christmas-time London derby. A 2-1 loss at Stamford Bridge comes after being one up after just four minutes before losing it in three second-half minutes with just a quarter of an hour to go.

The craziness of September is already behind us, October was great, November was good, and December is simply amazing.

Fulham beat CSKA 1-0 at home in the Europa League, reigniting hopes of advancing to the next stage, a target reached in the arctic weather of Basel. It's an afternoon game and the city of Basel is freezing. Our Super Whites play fearlessly and Bobby Zamora scores a quick-fire double just before half-time. Frei gets one back from the spot but Gera restores the two-goal cushion with only 13 minutes to go.

Basel just need a draw to progress so they were up for the fight and threw everything they had at Schwarzer and co., hitting the bar and scoring again in the 87th minute.

Dempsey doesn't have to regret his late miss as Fulham hold on and record an incredible achievement qualifying for the last 32. All this even without defensive leader Brede Hangeland.

In the Premier League, the first two December games come with minimum effort, maximum result: 1-0 by the river over Sunderland, 1-1 away at Burnley with Zamora scoring both for us.

Next to come are the visits of Manchester United and Tottenham, two games to be a little scared by possibly, but not this time. One of them even ends up on a DVD!

The afternoon of 19 December 2009 presents you with the chance to fully understand why football is so popular and gives out so many emotions.

Manchester United come down to London in a defensive emergency, needing to field the unusual duo of Darren Fletcher and Michael Carrick at the back, but still with players like Evra, Scholes, Rooney and Michael Owen in their starting XI and a bench featuring Berbatov, Danny Welbeck and Park Ji-sung.

Fulham take advantage and score three times: Murphy, who always likes to get one over Manchester United, an immense Zamora and the deserved prize for our Irish warrior Duff.

A smile still lights my face when I go back thinking about the scoreboard of the Cottage displaying Fulham 3 Manchester United 0 and all us singing 'Fergie, what's the score, Fergie, Fergie, what's the score?'

A week after that we come back from White Hart Lane with a point and a clean sheet but such a fantastic month definitely deserves a better end instead of the bitter one suffered at Chelsea.

Just before Christmas, the club also organise an open signing day at the stadium's shop. I go, exchanging words with the players, a really nice experience even if you're not a kid. Giovanni Pascoli, one of Italy's and the world's most famous poets, once said we should always keep the youth side alive inside us, and I'm definitely doing it with no shame at all.

Goosebumps are now flowing on my skin. Those first five months as a season ticket holder were just unrepeatable, so unique that it is really hard to find the right words to describe them if you've never been in that situation.

You feel part of something and especially in the UK where fans are so close to the pitch it really makes a difference and an impact on the game. And I was there. When I was going to the Stadio Romeo Menti to watch Vicenza, most of the time I was getting home voiceless but satisfied. If you're not a supporter, I'm sorry but I doubt you could get the real meaning of it. Some detractors say it's just a game but believe me, football really is not just a game.

Now that unfortunately business has to come first, owners, TV tycoons and sponsors should still think about supporters beforehand. Who buys merchandise? Who goes to the games? Who moves the economy with train tickets, flight bookings, hotels, pubs, restaurants and taxis?

Talk to a player now, when we've been unable to attend matches due to this damn virus, and he'll tell you how different it is playing in this situation and how better it is to play in a packed, loud, colourful stadium.

They would barely even celebrate a goal, whatever the importance of it. Most of the scorers still unconsciously run towards the stands after netting a goal. It's just automatic, you score – you run or look at the supporters to celebrate. That's it.

I'm a nobody to give out advice to multi-millionaires, super-powerful management companies, pay TV, yet I'm a supporter. I spend money, a lot usually, on kits, match tickets and travel, so, while I might sound naïve, please, don't forget that we're the ones who should come first.

The Rest Is History

Soundtrack: 'To Wish Impossible Things'
— The Cure

IF YOU dream, dream big! Would you tell me you've never placed a bet on Fulham winning the Premier League? Or that you were not among those who actually bet on us winning the 2010 Europa League?

The year 2010 sounds really like a big number, one of those used in the 1980s on fantasy, futuristic movie titles, and God only knows if 2010 wasn't an unpredictable, crazy, unforgettable year for all at Fulham Football Club.

It begins with a dramatic and horrific month of January during which the Whites lose all of their four league games. Astonishing. The calendar was tough as there were three away games out of the four fixtures but looking at the form the squad was in, it was really hard to predict a crash of these proportions.

Tony Pulis's Stoke City are not the best team to watch but they are a hard nut to break and a snowy night that previously benefited Fulham in Switzerland this time quickly looks like the worst nightmare as we go 3-0 down at the interval. The second half looks like another game, substitute Dempsey the star again assisting Duff and then scoring with a screamer from a long way out. Unfortunately it is not enough to at least recover a point. More than this though, the double 2-0 defeats at Blackburn and Aston Villa make Fulham bring back horror memories and look like a very average team. In between, another 2-0 debacle away to Spurs completes the pitiful hat-trick.

From an unbeaten December to a winless January, what really happened?

Fulham had already played a lot of games considering they started their European campaign back in July, and that the calendar of events was hectic, but January really surprised many.

February, the shortest month, was also packed with important games so they needed to be back on track to avoid ruining such a good first half of the season. And, thankfully, the players did just that.

This time there are three home games and two away, and the Cottagers record another unbeaten month in the Premier League.

Greening's goal is enough to see off Portsmouth in London before coming back from the tricky Reebok Stadium with a 0-0 draw. Two must-win games are then around the corner, Fulham hosting Burnley and Birmingham, and the boys deliver. A 3-0 mauling of the Clarets with even David Elm bagging a goal is followed by a last-minute 2-1 win over the Blues, after being one down. Zamora seals it in the 91st minute.

The trip to Sunderland produces another 0-0 draw and a good point to take back to London, and if the restored unbeaten run in the Premier League is not enough, there is also Europa League football to fit in a 28-day month. Fulham come up against Ukrainian superpower Shakhtar Donetsk, the reigning champions, in the round of 32.

Famously packed with Brazilian stars in the making, Shakhtar have in their ranks future Manchester City icon Fernandinho, future Chelsea and Arsenal genius Willian, future Bayern and Juventus sprinter Douglas Costa, well-travelled goal machine Luiz Adriano, 2008 Brazil Olympic gold medallist Ilsinho and Brazil 2013 Confederation Cup winner Jadson.

Top that with Croatia captain Darijo Srna and a few Russia and Ukraine internationals and you'll have an idea of what a team Shakhtar are.

In a 22,000-packed Craven Cottage, little Fulham rise to beat the champions 2-1 thanks to Gera and Zamora with Luiz Adriano having scored the momentary equaliser. But Mircea Lucescu's team don't take Zamora's form into account and when he blasts one of the goals of the tournament behind Andriy Pyatov's reach, a feeling starts growing even stronger inside us all. And the already famous 'Stand up if you still believe' chant becomes more than a simple song.

Just a week later, against all the odds, Fulham come away from the long trip to Donetsk with a 1-1 draw that qualifies them for the next round after an epic battle.

Hangeland's header puts the Cottagers in front, Jadson equalises, and Shakhtar at times look like a PlayStation globetrotter team. But Fulham hold on even after Murphy is sent off.

I remember former Juventus president Gianni Agnelli nicknaming Zbigniew Boniek 'Beauty of the Night' due to him performing well in European Cup games, maybe better than during normal league matches. Well, the Zoltán Gera I saw during that Europa League campaign really resembled that, because if every player stood out for Fulham that time, maybe Gera, Davies and Zamora even edged it a bit over the others.

So February goes with a brilliant set of games to find inspiration from for new battles. That unfortunately doesn't happen in March as Fulham lose all three Premier League games, showing again a particular annoying allergy to travelling.

Manchester this time is stingy with us and the two trips over there see the Whites coming back with 3-0 and 2-1 defeats to United and City respectively.

Hull again means trouble for us and we lose 2-0 with former Craven Cottage favourite Jimmy Bullard scoring against us.

But despite that, the disastrous Premier League form of March is forgotten about because of Fulham's form in the Europa League.

Awaiting the over-achieving Whites in the round of 16 are Juventus, a true world superpower and my first love. My Juventus. Incredible.

Back in my Vicenza days, we faced Juventus a few times in Serie A. I had always gone for Vicenza. First of all because I've been actively supporting and watching them much more than Juventus, and Turin is a four-hour drive from my house. Then because Juventus could most of the time do without the points, which were instead always very valuable to Vicenza.

And the same was going to happen in this case.

A couple of good friends and two of my French cousins were coming to see me so I secured tickets for everybody. My friend was another big Juve fan but my cousins were definitely going for Fulham, especially as one of them was a huge *Milanista*[3].

Before that, though, Fulham have to travel to the Stadio Delle Alpi for the first leg. A star-studded Juventus, even going through one of their glorious history's most difficult times (after being relegated and title-stripped due to the *Calciopoli* affair), dominate us, winning 3-1, and Etuhu's deflected goal was a really lucky gift to preserve carefully.

Almost 24,000 people attend the return game; Juventus are favourites and probably only we believed Fulham could turn that deficit around. I was telling everybody that it would not

---

3   AC Milan supporter

be a walk in the park and that I was confident Fulham would go through as I knew that the Cottage would help. I've lived the atmosphere there; I knew we could do that.

Unfortunately, very few people trusted my words.

Roy Hodgson makes some changes, fielding the eclectic Chris Baird in central midfield with Etuhu, Murphy being suspended, and Stephen Kelly at right-back.

Not long after kick-off, captain David Trezeguet, one of the Juve players I've always liked, pokes a loose ball in for 1-0 on the night. A goal so early, putting Juve 4-1 up on aggregate and equalising the ever-important away goal tally, would have killed anybody. But not Fulham, not us in the stands. 'Stand up if you still believe' resounds high and loud.

It takes just six minutes for Zamora to show Italy's World Cup-winning captain Fabio Cannavaro that it's going to be a much tougher night than expected when he overpowers the defender and then smashes in the equaliser. The Cottage explodes with joy. 'Ohhh, Bobby Zamora.'

Golden-kitted Juventus look shaky, Fulham press high, and Zamora plays a through ball to Gera who is downed by Cannavaro. A red card quickly follows.

Bobby forces a good save from Chimenti from the following free kick and minutes later Simon Davies hits the bar from another set piece. Then comes a corner and Etuhu hits the post with a header.

Juventus are battered by a spirited Fulham. A magic pass from Zamora sees Davies square the ball for Gera who anticipates Grosso, another World Cup hero, and makes it 2-1. This is going beyond fantasy and dreams; everybody is jumping, celebrating and embracing friends or even simple strangers within reach.

When the referee blows for half-time it's Juventus who incredibly look like a boxer saved by the bell.

But unfortunately for them Fulham come back like a wolf smelling blood and with only four minutes on the clock in the second half Diego's handball in the box means a penalty for the Whites. Gera steps up looking so calm that he almost frightens me but he scores – 3-1 to Fulham, the tie is now even, and we only need one more goal to progress.

I imagine some bookies going through the odds to calculate how much it will cost them if Fulham could miraculously win it.

Time goes on though and that goal doesn't come with Chimenti making a couple of good saves. Dempsey, often sacrificed recently to the new 4-4-1-1 formation, comes on the pitch with 20 minutes to go but there are only eight left when the improbable happens.

The ball is passed on the edge of the box between Fulham's players. Etuhu lobs it for Dempsey who takes it down, turns and with a moment of magic only top players own, chips the ball towards the far corner. Chimenti this time can just watch in disbelief as it ends up in the net. Hodgson is amazed and the Cottage united as one.

'And it has lifted the roof of the old place' is a line of commentary that perfectly described the scene and every time I watch the highlights it puts a smile on my face and warms my heart up.

There's still time for Zebina, who I never really liked, to be red-carded for kicking Duff from the back. I only feel for Del Piero, who definitely cared more than others even being on the bench.

I am over the moon at an epic victory. Yes, Fulham were the first club founded in London but had no trophies in the cabinet, if we forget about the Intertoto Cup and a few lower-division titles, so to beat such a European giant is simply amazing. I have some mixed feelings too though, legitimately

I'd say. The Old Lady[4] had always been my team, I celebrated Champions League and Club World Cup victories, but now they were going through some hard times after rebuilding following their relegation to Serie B. To crash like that against 'little' Fulham would mean further criticism and plenty of mockery from rival fans in Italy and that saddened me a bit.

But they have all the resources to get back where they belong and today is Fulham's day. What a story; Fulham beat Juventus 5-4 on aggregate and are now in the quarter finals of a European competition. Please don't wake me up.

'I told you' is a phrase that has always annoyed me but this time I was quite happy to dispense it towards all people who laughed at me when I said Fulham would go through. Lesson learned, my friends.

---

4   Juventus's nickname

One of a Kind

Soundtrack: 'Shine On You Crazy Diamond'
– Pink Floyd

TIME TO celebrate, not just for Fulham, as my great friend Umberto is back in town! He didn't last much in Italy, I reckon he's made for London.

To have him back is wonderful, I laugh so much in his company because he's simply crazy, in the nicest way. I just love spending time with him.

One day we are at the cinema with another good friend, Federico, to see *The Girl with the Dragon Tattoo*. We sit down, the movie begins, and it's in Swedish with English subtitles. Federico asks, 'But, it's in Swedish, we have to follow the subs?' Umberto, as cool as ever, replies 'You have to, I speak fluent Swedish.' A little silence and we all start laughing.

Around Easter in 2010, I'm hanging out with a girl who works in my same building. We frequently meet during breaks and a full floor still unoccupied means we can have fun enjoying the view over Hammersmith, happy days.

We are in bed at my place when I receive a text from Umberto, 'Have you got plans for tomorrow?' I explain the situation and he laughs, 'Okay, no problem, it happens I've two tickets for United–Chelsea, but if you're busy I'll ask somebody else.'

Now is my turn to laugh and I tell him to count me in and we will meet at 7am. I talk to the girl, she's not that happy to leave but hey, the first thing she did once she got in was to perfectly pile my CDs and fold my jumper. Sorry, but that's not the right move for the very first time you come home. I kiss her goodbye and have dinner with Mr Cook who laughs when I tell him the story.

Umberto picks me up by Balham station, in his boss's Jaguar. I am already thinking it's going to be another crazy day. We stop somewhere in the Midlands for a bite to eat then continue up to Old Trafford.

The 'asshole' only tells me once we are there that we have to watch the game in the away end. Ahhhh come on, if he was anybody else I'd kick his ass, but he's Umbe, so I laugh and get ready for a long couple of hours.

Chelsea win 2-1 with Joe Cole and Didier Drogba scoring. My countryman Federico Macheda gets one back for the Red Devils and I have to control myself because I'm among enemies.

We hit the road again and I tell Umberto he's forgiven because I love his being crazy like that, and we laugh.

After a few hours we're back in London. We get out and he takes a deep breath, 'Now I can tell you we didn't have the spare wheel.' Jeeeez. I put my arm on my forehead and go. I reckon I keep on laughing on my own for the entire walk until the tube.

Umberto died of leukaemia on 8 July 2014.

I was proud to have managed to take Umberto to the Cottage at least once. We had fun, plenty of beers and he was an instant hit with my Fulham mates. He was definitely one of a kind. Marina O'Loughlin, the famous restaurant critic, loved him and was always giving riveting reviews about him when visiting places he used to manage around London. The *Steeple Times* website dedicated a profile to him in its Characters feature, saying, 'You won't meet a maître d' like him. Scomparin does a mean Liverpudlian impression and following a stint at the now defunct Ilia, he's moving on to pastures new. An evening in his company is always going to be jolly.'

Umberto was the best brother you'd wish for even without being my blood brother.

When I Feared Everything Was About to Come Down

Soundtrack: 'It Takes a Fool to Remain Sane'
– The Ark

THE PREVIOUS year I was considering whether to stay or not in London. I missed the sun and a few good friends back home were getting in touch about doing some business together. Well, after the Juve game I thought back about it and was I happy I stayed!

For the next few days I reckon I was going around feeling like I was more handsome, bigger, almost untouchable. I'm crazy, I know, but that's the effect something as big as that can give you.

I was very happy because Clint Dempsey scored the final goal and especially in that way, showing the world what he was capable of. He was and still is my favourite Fulham player of all time. He was not very fast, nor hugely gifted, but was so passionate and proud, always giving 100 per cent and he got better and better. And that doesn't happen overnight or just ageing in a barrel like a good wine; no, that comes with a lot of training, sacrifice and strong will.

Back in the Premier League, Fulham begin April with possibly our most common score, 2-1, beating Wigan at the

Cottage. Hangeland and Stefano Okaka, a January signing and goalscorer against us in Rome only a few months ago, overturn an initial disadvantage.

The Whites then continue adding points with good 0-0 draws at Anfield and at home to Wolves, while they close a month again with a defeat, a painful one at that, 2-1 at Goodison Park with Arteta winning it for Everton in the 94th minute after Nevland had put us in front in the first half. A word beginning with F comes to mind.

On 1 April Fulham play host to VfL Wolfsburg for the first leg of the Europa League quarter-final.

First the reigning Europa League champions, then the Italian Old Lady, now the defending German Bundesliga champions. As usual, we are the underdogs.

The Germans have an attack of Edin Džeko, prior to his big move to Manchester City, along with Brazilian Grafite who scored 28 goals in 25 games during the title-winning season and former Newcastle striker Obafemi Martins. In their ranks are also Fulham-to-be Ashkan Dejagah and Sascha Riether, while Swiss international keeper Diego Benaglio is in goal.

In a quick-fire four minutes in the second half, Zamora and Duff put Fulham in the driving seat at 2-0, and nothing else really happens until the 89th minute when after a corner Madlung heads in for Wolfsburg and leaves all of us gobsmacked.

Fulham have made the quarter-finals against every possible prediction and were in charge against the German champions, but 2-1 is a completely different score to take to Saxony. However, if you had asked any Fulham fan if they'd have taken a 2-1 victory they'd probably have said yes.

For the second leg a week later, in a city where Volkswagen has its headquarters, it is clear from the big screens inside the stadium – showing wolves ready to hunt – that the Germans are ready to fight tooth and nail.

But the marvellous Zamora only needs 20 seconds to tame those wolves. He receives a low pass inside the box and flicks it with his heel, fooling another Italian World Cup winner in Andrea Barzagli, and easily scores. A 1-0 win for Fulham on the night is enough for 3-1 on aggregate and a place in the semi-finals.

Semi-finals, mental, history, whatever you might want to call it. Fulham will play another German colossus, Hamburger Sport-Verein, HSV, or simply Hamburg. The oldest club in Germany had been founded in 1887, eight years after us.

Before another date with history though, there's time for my usual Easter break away with Giampaolo and our mates, and we head to Kiev.

Besides being the homeland of the most beautiful girls in the world, because literally 999 out of 1,000 are models, we also find the time for a football game.

It's derby day in the Ukrainian capital, Dynamo Kyiv v Arsenal Kyiv.

The football isn't the highest quality but it's a couple of hours of fun with the boys. Former superstar and Chelsea misfit Andriy Shevchenko is playing for the hosts.

Once back in London, the game I care for is next. Just a fortnight later Fulham are again in Germany hoping it won't be their last visit as the final is scheduled to be played at the pretty new Imtech Arena. Hamburg would love to play the final on home soil.

At this point, Hamburg have a trophy list that could scare anybody: six Bundesligas, three German Cups, two League Cups, one European Cup, one European Cup Winners' Cup, two Intertoto Cups and a proud history of never having been relegated.

Not that Fulham seem to care much about opponents' history or fame, and they also have the advantage of playing the second leg at home.

The Whites once more face a line-up full of big names: Jerome Boateng, Zé Roberto, Mathijsen, Petrić, Guerrero and the unforgotten Ruud van Nistelrooy. And the Londoners would also have to travel by road as British airspace is closed down.

On the other hand, they can also field their best XI with Baird at right-back, the strong Murphy–Etuhu partnership in the middle and Gera just off Zamora.

It's almost all Hamburg and I'm suffering a lot in front of the TV with Mark Schwarzer our MVP by a mile, but the night finishes goalless. Zamora goes off injured and a 1-1 draw in the second leg will qualify the Germans. It was always going to be tough and now it had got even tougher.

By Thursday, 29 April, I am as excited as ever in my seat at the most beautiful ground in the world, Craven Cottage. It's packed and I can see from my fellow fans' eyes that we believe it's going to be another great night.

Paintsil is back and it's the only change. Zamora, nursing an Achilles injury, starts and with how vital he has been, he couldn't be left out. Dempsey is on the bench while Hamburg present Mladen Petrić up front with Guerrero being dropped.

The Germans start the better with something to prove after sacking their manager over the weekend. Attacking the Hammersmith End, left-footed Croatian international Petrić takes a free kick and unleashes a fierce shot that crashes in perfectly at the right-hand corner. For a moment, silence is the loudest noise in the stadium. From behind the goal I saw its fabulous trajectory. Hamburg's players are celebrating, not only because it was a screamer, but also because they have got the away goal they need.

Chants resume and the Whites need us now more than possibly ever. We still believe, and we make it clear, but the first half ends with Hamburg 1-0 up and if the night finishes like that, they will be in the final.

Zamora is again subbed within ten minutes of the second half starting, Dempsey comes on, and Duff almost equalises.

In the 69th minute Murphy plays a perfect through ball for Simon Davies who gets possessed by the spirit of Messi, makes a fool of Demel and beats Rost to equalise. I, instead, get possessed by the spirit of some random nutter and I run down the stadium stairs screaming and waving my arms. Fulham are level and it's total pandemonium. I swear the columns are moving!

Seven minutes later we win a corner. Davies plays it straight into the box and with Demel still staring, the cross goes off him and runs loose. Saint Zoltán Gera from Pecs is first on it, like those vigilant condors waiting for the right moment to attack their preys, and quickly turns and puts it in. YEEEEE EEEEEEESSSSSSSSSSSSSSSSSSSSSSSSSS. Delirium all over and I embrace every person who comes within reach. I shout, I jump, and I can't believe it.

Craven Cottage is coming down, I'm sure this time, and the echoes of our screams are testing the old place's solidity to a different level.

Hamburg are now dead and buried, and it's all Fulham before the final whistle sparks wild celebrations. 'And now you've got to believe it, a night beyond compare.' The commentator's words said it all.

Roy Hodgson tries to go back to regular respiration, Paintsil runs the length of the pitch while other Fulham players switch between consoling opponents and hugs with team-mates.

I take a deep breath. My heart was pumping strongly with pure happiness. The stands are emptying slowly because almost nobody wants to leave. I'd stay here all night if possible, soaking in the magic and fulfilling atmosphere. Fulham are once more re-writing history and we're part of it. I'm part of it.

Players and staff leave the pitch under another round of well-deserved applause which they proudly return; stewards say it's time to go. Just before getting out I turn and look at the stadium structure. I bet the iron, steel, plastic and wood are also relieved the game has finished.

We're in the final. Wow.

The fresh air of London by night caresses my face while a chuffed smile stays with me until I get home. Mr Cook is sincerely happy and greets me with joy. We have a little chat then I get to my room. I set the alarm knowing that I'm going to sleep heavy. No dreams tonight, they just came true.

Winners Take It All

Soundtrack: 'About Today' – The National

SECURING SAFETY is no longer a problem with Fulham now an established, well-respected Premier League club on the rise, and we start the month of May by beating West Ham 3-2 with a good display. Dempsey scores the opener and Okaka gets the winner, either side of an own goal.

It's a pity that we then lose the remaining two games as it could have been another top-ten finish.

Stoke complete the double against us with a 1-0 win at the Cottage while Arsenal respond to their early-season loss with a thumping 4-0 at the Emirates. The Whites end in 12th after 12 wins, ten draws and 16 defeats for a total of 46 points.

In May, though, there's a place for only one game in everybody's heads: the Europa League Final 12 days into the month. Maybe even at the club they didn't think the team could reach such a target and getting a ticket becomes a little challenging. Eventually, season ticket holders can purchase up to six tickets. I secure mine, sending all details also for the bus seat.

I haven't been to many away games with Vicenza, Juventus or Fulham. So far seen the Cottagers in quite a few London derbies, this year twice at White Hart Lane – once in the Premier League, then for the FA Cup replay.

Once inside White Hart Lane, the view is great. From the outside it resembles a shopping centre to me but now it's a cool, modern ground.

I have been to the Emirates, Stamford Bridge and Upton Park. But this is a European final! I've emailed my boss to take the day off with a view on having the following one too.

I hear older Fulham supporters talk about how far the club has gone since the days they used to gather at Craven Cottage to go to places like Torquay or Carlisle in the lower divisions but they are now waiting for the bus which will take them to a European final.

I envy them a bit. In the end England is football's birthplace and every club, even from the smaller towns, has an amazing tale to go back to, especially the FA Cup tradition of unknown minnows with the chance to one day face a superpower.

We move through London lights on the way to Folkestone where we will get the Channel Tunnel to Calais.

I'm almost at the back of the bus when somebody asks me if I could swap the seat so a couple can be reunited. I've no problem at all. She's all smiles and I'm at the very back where I meet Jeff, Mark and Ben. We start chatting and they're very pleased and probably proud that an Italian guy in London supports Fulham. And I'm also very proud that they appreciate it. We get on immediately and keep on chatting for a while.

With customs formalities behind us, we hit the road again for Hamburg. The night swallows up and the bus is silent. I also fall asleep.

I wonder how many of us are dreaming of tomorrow's game.

The trip is long and tiring but I found a way to rest and I'm buzzing as we finally reach Hamburg. The bus stops, somebody stretches out and someone else lights a desired cigarette. I can now see how huge Ben is while Jeff and Mark are more of my size.

In the other semi-final, Atlético Madrid beat Liverpool so the final won't be an all-English affair. Plenty of Colchoneros are also colouring the streets and they're also loud and excited. Beer starts flowing and I quickly decide that British ales are way better than German lagers and Pils. Then comes the song, 'We are Fulham, we are Fulham, we are Fulham, FFC. We are Fulham, super Fulham, we are Fulham, fuck Chelsea!'

It's an incredible atmosphere and being here is a privilege. I speak to some Spanish fans and they reckon this is going to be their easiest win. Should I remind them what happened to the Juve fans who told me the same in March?

Some say they respect Fulham, and some didn't even know us prior to this game. I gain their sympathy for expressing my disliking for Real Madrid and that I came from Vicenza, where they also play in a red-and-white-striped shirt similar to Atlético.

There's so much beer, drinks and words going around that we lose hold of time and so we have to run to the ground. Damn, I missed the kick-off, a thing that really annoys me!

Anyway, here we are. Atlético's starting XI is simply terrifying.

David de Gea in goal, Antonio López, Tomáš Ujfaluši, Álvaro Dominguez and Luis Perea the back four, Raúl García and Paulo Assunção in the middle, Simão Sabrosa and José Antonio Reyes wide, Diego Forlán and Sergio Agüero up front. Just by reading it you can understand how uneven this game was on paper.

Fulham field their season's best XI: Mark Schwarzer, Chris Baird, Brede Hangeland, Aaron Hughes, Paul Konchesky, Simon Davies, Danny Murphy, Dickson Etuhu, Damien Duff, with Zoltán Gera just off Bobby Zamora. Unfortunately neither Zamora nor substitute Clint Dempsey is 100 per cent fit.

Atlético Madrid play in their classic striped kit, while we're in our third kit, a cool navy blue.

The atmosphere is great, and I like a lot the fact that fans can put up flags and pennants. Atlético's supporters have a huge red and white banner which almost takes over their end.

It's clear from the beginning that Atlético will be in charge and Fulham will try to take advantage of pauses in the game. Murphy unusually gives away the ball in our half, Agüero steals it and cuts it through for Forlán a few steps forward. He shoots but the base of the post deflects it out for Schwarzer's and, probably even more, Murphy's relief.

Davies responds with a nice volley that goes straight into De Gea's gloves. Then the Colchoneros take the lead.

Reyes charges forward on the flank and squares the ball in the middle for Simão who flicks it for Agüero. The Argentine star mis-kicks the ball and unluckily for Fulham that's the best thing he can do as it becomes the perfect assist for his striking partner Forlán, who poaches in while almost offside. One half of the ground erupts in glory.

Just five minutes later, though, Zamora does his best at defending the ball and getting into the box. The chance looks gone as Atlético players swarm back in. Baird crosses, the ball is headed towards Davies who again volleys it with class, beating De Gea in the corner. YEEEEEEEEEEEEEEEESSSSSSSSSSSSSS COME ON! This time our end goes bonkers. We're alive, Fulham are in the game, respect is due to an honestly stronger opponent but the game has to be played and then we'll see the outcome.

For the third time in a row Dempsey comes in for Zamora within ten minutes of the second half starting. Our big boy bit the bullet to be here but he's clearly in pain and not at his best. Atlético also make two changes, refreshing their attack with José Manuel Jurado and Eduardo Salvio. Another two big names.

The game goes on and Davies tests De Gea again, then Agüero puts a shot wide from close range. Both teams are now on guard and not risking much as extra time approaches, Nevland coming in for Duff.

It's not a spectacular game but more a tense fencing battle. Fulham's players are queueing up for a massage. The incredibly long season has taken its toll and there's at least another 30 minutes to be played.

Atlético are livelier with the South American strikers bossing our defence. Fulham resist though, Schwarzer makes a good save, and Agüero again pokes wide.

I reckon that if I had the habit of biting my nails I'd be fingerless by now.

Penalties are looming and I'm considering who'd take ours with specialists like Zamora and Duff off the pitch. I'm dreaming of maybe unsung hero Baird winning the cup for us. What a story that would be.

Then, just four minutes away from the Russian roulette, Agüero squares a low ball into the box, and Forlán as usual comes in first but doesn't kick it properly. This time though the stars take a nap, the ball bounces on Hangeland's big boot and agonisingly scrambles in.

Our end is now like an abandoned Arctic land where it is cold and silent and there's no place for emotions. I'm speechless.

The referee blows the whistle, Atlético's players celebrate while my beloved Fulham ones crash on the pitch, exhausted and drained, not only physically. Our opponents' end is a carnival and I envy them a lot. Atlético are a great club with lots of trophies, so why couldn't the skies leave this to us? We will probably have to wait decades again, if we're lucky enough, to have another chance like this.

The Spaniards leave chanting and buzzing, ready to hit the city and drink the victory up. My fellow Fulham fans leave upset and perturbed. The Imtech Arena slowly loses its heart and falls asleep, while I find myself leaning on the stand's protection, my scarf covering my head as I don't want to be seen so sad.

Mr Cook texts me to say that British TV showed Lily Allen in tears, a saddened Hugh Grant and then me. I didn't realise I was almost the only one still in.

I'm so down I feel weak. I leave the ground and the streets are a multitude of red, white and blue jubilant Atlético fans. Some come by to congratulate us as Fulham were a much tougher nut to break than they thought.

I bet sangria, tinto del verano and calimocho[5] are flooding Madrid. Back in the Spanish capital it must be party time with also plenty of San Miguel and Mahou[6] involved, while in London pints of ale are probably used to tame sadness.

I catch up with Jeff, Mark and Ben, who also have no desire to talk. We get on the bus and the air is heavy and charged with negativity. Understandable. It's been like reading a fairytale, getting the taste of it and just waiting for the happy ending only to find out on the very last page that the beloved protagonist dies or that the couple, formed through difficulties and rival families, can't eventually get married.

The route back to London seems infinite. We get off by Putney Bridge, I exchange numbers with my new mates and then send a message to Antonio saying I'm not going into work today.

I reach Balham; Mr Cook hands me a cup of coffee and listens to my outburst, which I really appreciate. His wisdom

---

5   Typical Spanish wine cocktails
6   Spanish beers from Madrid

is so helpful and he makes me realise how proud I should be instead of being sad. I should be grateful that I was part of something almost unrepeatable. Pride should be the emotion; little Fulham beat some of Europe's finest, reached a European final with a club budget possibly ten, 20 times smaller than their opponents'.

Thanks, Mr Cook, I see things differently now. Of course my heart is still broken and it will take time to forget we were so close to this amazing achievement, but yes, we should be so proud of our players, our manager and everybody involved. I'm very relieved, I go upstairs, take a shower and then crash in bed.

When I eventually wake up in the afternoon, I still have that bitter taste in my mouth but my heart feels so much better. I had the fortune to see Fulham reach such an important final, England's only team to go that far this year. Liverpool were eliminated in the semis and there were no English teams in the Champions League last four.

Inter Milan winning the Champions League and doing the treble really makes the year much worse, but let's stick with Fulham, super Fulham, proud finalists of the 2010 Europa League.

And it's such a pity there's no more Premier League games to play because it would have been great to pay a well-deserved homage to our boys, greeting them in a packed Craven Cottage singing their names.

You wrote history, guys, you'll always be remembered in our hearts!

Sparks

Soundtrack: 'My Way' – Frank Sinatra

WE COULD stay here forever talking about Roy Hodgson's decision to leave Fulham and take the vacant job at Liverpool. Right choice? Wrong choice? Time will show it to be the wrong move, but could you blame him at the time?

I didn't. I got to love him for how far he took us and for coming in during a very tough time. He had the balls to do it, stood strong and drove us out of the darkness while restoring pride and honour to the club.

On 29 July 2010, former Manchester United and Barcelona star Mark Hughes is appointed as the new Fulham manager. He comes in after managing Blackburn and Manchester City, where oil money has now started pumping the club to a higher level.

Hughes is renowned for being a tough guy who likes his team to try to play football. That is enough for me.

The transfer window is quiet, after a couple of years of massive turn-arounds. Philippe Senderos joins from Arsenal, Jonathan Greening is rightly rewarded with a new contract while Mexican international left-back Carlos Salcido comes in from Dutch giants PSV Eindhoven. Also signed from the Eredivisie is AZ midfielder Moussa Dembélé for £5m. Algerian centre-back Rafik Halliche joins from Portuguese giants

Benfica and two young prospects, Finland's Lauri Dalla Valle and Sweden's Alexander Kačaniklić, plus money are swapped for Paul Konchesky who follows Hodgson to Liverpool.

Fulham then make a huge profit by selling former unknown Chris Smalling to Manchester United for an eight-figure sum while I'm personally very sad to see Erik Nevland go. He played a key role in our great escape and was one of our many unsung heroes.

The new season's schedule is officially out and I'm so looking forward to going back to Craven Cottage.

The chance comes when for one of the pre-season friendlies Fulham play another German giant, Werder Bremen, and come out 5-1 victors after Pizarro gave the lead to the visitors in the first half only for Gera to score a hat-trick in the second.

The new season kicks off on 14 August and the Whites come back from the Reebok Stadium with a 0-0 draw. David Stockdale deputised for Schwarzer in the only change from the Hodgson era.

The first home game is a tough one as we host Manchester United. It's another classic, a 2-2 draw with Hangeland the unexpected star, scoring an 84th- minute own goal and making amend, just five minutes later to seal the second draw in a row.

The last game of the month sees us travelling to newly promoted Blackpool, and it's goals galore part two. Another 2-2 draw sees Zamora put us in front and an 87th-minute goal by Etuhu wins us a point. We have to wait until our fourth game of the season to get our first win and why not do so with our beloved 2-1 score?

New signing Dembélé steals the show with an impressive display, scoring a brace to win it against a foul-happy Wolverhampton Wanderers. We keep the unbeaten start with two draws, away to Blackburn and at home to Everton.

The game at Ewood Park is almost another rugby match with Rovers playing a very physical style which many times seeks out an unnecessary tackle. Dempsey scores and we take a very well-deserved point back to London. On the bus there's a quiz on Fulham history. The prize is our third kit special edition in Harrods' colours, green and gold. And, yes, I won it.

An in-form Dempsey scores again at Upton Park where we take another point. He's fit and feeling Sparky's trust so he delivers. Hodgson at times was too conservative and Dempsey had to be parked on the bench. Mind you, Gera did amazingly well, and he was a bit luckier to stay fit for longer.

With my new friends Jeff, Mark and Ben, we enjoy another great day out at West Ham with the excuse of celebrating a rare point at the Boleyn.

The club then organise an open training session in October so fans can go and enjoy a day out at Motspur Park with the chance to interact with manager and players. It's a good opportunity and I decide to go as I haven't seen our training facilities yet.

It is super easy to get there from Balham so I grab my camera, put on my jacket and off I go. It's an incredibly nice and sunny day for the end of October. Somebody from the staff welcomes us and lets us enjoy a coffee or a tea once inside the facilities.

Players arrive and start training together with Hughes's coaches. We were told we could ask questions to the gaffer so I'm looking forward to meeting him.

The boss arrives, gives a brief speech and then answers some questions. I ask him why Paintsil is playing less under him and I feel like he doesn't like me asking about it. He politely replies though, Paints needs to keep working hard and he'll play.

Is that how you define 'politically correct'?

Other spectators ask questions, the gaffer shares his thoughts and then agrees to some pics with us.

It was a great day out. I love these things and I reckon Fulham perfectly know how to make you feel like it's a big family.

Back to playing time and after all those positive results, our beloved 2-1 score punishes us twice in a row. After losing the home derby against Spurs, having gone in front, we repeated the feat a week later at West Brom.

Dempsey's brace gets us back to winning ways though as the last game of October is won at home to Wigan. Thanks again for the birthday present!

We have a little celebration with my house-mates and Giampaolo joins in later on as he had a date through an online dating website. He's over the moon, he keeps on mentioning this stunning Gill he has just met.

He asks what he should text her, he's as usual being so funny and clumsy. I'm happy we got back at being best mates after a few months in which we didn't talk much.

I went out with a girl he was dating long before. I'd told him I wanted to and he said he was okay with it but eventually he wasn't and we fell out. But there's an old saying in Italy, 'Women pass, friendship stays.'

In November we scrap a home point in the 90th minute versus Villa, thanks to Hangeland, before annoyingly losing again in the Fulham Road derby at Stamford Bridge.

We come away with a point in the 0-0 draw at Newcastle before receiving a hard football lesson at the Cottage from Hughes's former team, Manchester City. That first-half performance is one of the nicest and most incredible display, of free-flowing, attacking football I've ever seen live.

The Whites are taken apart by a team fielding Yaya Touré, David Silva and Carlos Tevez, supported by Gareth Barry and

Nigel De Jong. Even misfit Jô looks like a great player. Roberto Mancini's men are a pleasure to watch and I remember being quite relieved we were only 3-0 down at the interval.

In the following game, Dempsey scores once more in the disappointing 1-1 home draw to Birmingham.

Things are not great and on 4 December, Umberto invites me to the Emirates to watch Arsenal v Fulham as one of his clients is giving him a couple of season tickets.

I've already been there but a day with Umbe is always worth it. This time I'm not among crooks turned supporters and instead we get a comfortable grandstand seat between more civilised people.

The Gunners are really doing well and it's going to be hard to get anything. Samir Nasri, unfortunately for us, is in the form of his life this season and scores two brilliant goals so, even if Fulham did play well and Kamara initially equalised, Arsenal win it 2-1.

They go top of the league; we're just avoiding the W-filled relegation zone – Wigan, West Ham and Wolves – thanks to a better goal difference than the Latics.

Thankfully, Umberto's company and some pints of Guinness help cheer me up.

Initial enthusiasm makes space for old fears when we draw 0-0 at home to Sunderland. Quite a few fans are moaning from the stands and it is not the best farewell for me.

I've already told Antonio that I'll be going back to Italy for good this Christmas. A couple of interesting business options with some friends are on the table and I sadly have to say goodbye to London. Again.

Before going though, I purchase a ticket for our visit to Anfield on 18 December. I'm very excited and looking forward to hearing live the famous 'You'll Never Walk Alone' for the first time and hopefully taking some points away from the Kop.

It's another very cold winter and some snow has begun falling down while I approach the quiet of Craven Cottage in the early morning. I take a seat on the bus and start reading something when the rumour breaks; it has been snowing heavily in Liverpool since last night and there are fears the game could be called off. No way! Come on, it's my last game for quite a long time and it can't go like this!

Fulham FC personnel advise that some other games are being called off due to stadium areas being dangerous because of the frozen surfaces. My sixth sense doesn't give me good feelings about the situation and promptly we hear the unwanted news that the game is indeed off.

I curse every single saint I can and hit the road in a very bad mood. No Anfield, no game.

On 20 December 2010 my second London life comes to an end and I fly home packed with memories and mixed emotions, knowing I was going to miss London. I see Mr Cook crying as the taxi takes me away from Balham. I'm doing the same and I'm so lost I forget I still have the house keys with me so we have to make a U-turn.

I'll never forget all the good times I had in this house and all the special people I met. Mr Cook is a true friend and a person I still keep in my heart. He really acted like a second father for me.

I managed to take Wendy and Phil with me to the Cottage once for the family and friends day, when a ticket for the game was just a tenner. They had a lot of fun and Wendy from time to time reminds me of that day and I know Phil has now sympathy for the Whites!

Even big Kieran, an Irish guy who lived there for a while, much more a rugby man than a football fan, cheers for Fulham now. Goodbye London, I'm sure we'll see each other again. Hopefully soon.

Family is the best way to comfort me and brighten up my mood. It's Christmas, I'm home, and it really helps. Two days in and Antonio calls me from the office. The owner of the company just realised that maybe I was very important and he's offering me a higher position with much, much more money. FFS! Why did you not do that last week or when Antonio told you I was leaving?!

It's too late. I have made my mind up. Antonio had some hopes but unfortunately my answer is no. Antonio is another person who will stay in my life, we became good friends, and we went through all phases of the company and honestly did an amazing job.

The first thing I do once back is subscribe to Sky Sport (Italy). Fulham pick up my thoughts and win 2-0 away to Stoke thanks to Bairdinho's brace, one of those a proper rocket.

Gareth Bale wins the home match for Tottenham on 1 January but the boys immediately bounce back, thumping West Brom 3-0 by the river with Dempsey again on the score sheet.

Hughes likes to rotate his players around the defensive duo of Hangeland and Aaron Hughes, and the midfield pair of Murphy and Etuhu. Dempsey is the usual choice up front with Gera, Johnson and Kamara rotating when Zamora is not fit. Baird's adaptability to different roles sees him playing frequently; all defensive and midfield positions are okay for this incredible utility player. Salcido and Halliche are failing for the moment to adjust to the Premier League but Dembélé is showing his crystal-clear class.

An away draw at Wigan and another home brace by Dempsey are enough to complete the double over Stoke, meaning seven points in three games for the Whites. They unfortunately surrender to Liverpool when the famous postponed game is eventually played, 1-0 with an unlucky own goal by Paintsil.

Watching games on TV is really not the same as being there but I have to get used to it again now.

Duff scores against his former employers when Fulham edge past the visiting Newcastle to open February in the right way. The month sees the boys drawing the other three games. A 0-0 home stalemate to Chelsea came in between a 2-2 at Aston Villa and a 1-1 at Manchester City. Paintsil scores another own goal, Dempsey keeps on improving his tally, and Duff bags the point against the Cityzens.

Diomansy Kamara then goes out on loan to Leicester City – another one of my favourite players leaving the club.

A spirited Blackburn are tamed 3-2 thanks to returning Zamora who coolly converts a 90th-minute penalty to send the Cottage wild. Duff continues his scoring form with a good brace.

I like what I see. Hodgson and Hughes have had two different visions; maybe more conservative the first, a bit more modern the latter. So far I'm happy with Hughes's appointment.

Dempsey bags another goal, this time sadly irrelevant, as my former idol Louis Saha has already won it for Everton at Goodison Park, 2-1.

Zamora's brace and Etuhu's rare effort are enough to see off Blackpool, 3-0 at the Cottage, before Fulham again come away empty-handed from the Theatre of Dreams, losing 2-0 to Manchester United with the game already decided in the first half.

Sparky's men have character and bag another seven points in three games. First is a 1-1 draw at Molineux, and then an unusual 3-0 double over Bolton and at Sunderland. Dempsey gets another brace, Davies has one while new loan signing Gael Kakuta opens the scoring at Sunderland.

The last three games of the season are to everybody's tastes: a 5-2 defeat by Liverpool, a 2-0 win away to Birmingham with

Hangeland scoring both, then a 2-2 home draw in the closing game with Arsenal. Youngster Theo Walcott ruins our party in the 89th minute.

This is my first match since leaving London. It's such a great feeling to be back among friends like the crazy trio of Jeff, Mark and Ben, who also teach me a new drinking game.

Fulham finish eighth with 11 wins, 11 defeats, 16 draws and 49 points. Hughes's first season can be called a success even if Bolton have kicked the Whites out of the FA Cup in the fifth round after we had smashed Spurs 4-0 in one of the best performances of the year.

Hughes resigns in early June, claiming he has ambitions to fulfil; Al-Fayed defines him as a strange man. Personally it saddens me to see things going this way; we were on the rise and even if both men have strong personalities, I see this as an actual turning point. We'll unfortunately realise its magnitude only in times to come.

It's Never Too Late

Soundtrack: 'Mr Writer' – Stereophonics

THE EVENTUAL appointment of Martin Jol has raised many an eyebrow in doubt, I'm sure. Speculation linked him as Roy Hodgson's replacement, but it didn't happen and Hughes came in. Now Jol has signed.

Was Sparky's appointment a temporary solution since the beginning then? I think that probably many fans would agree there.

Anyway, there's no time to debate on this, the new season is not so far away and a new manager often means new strategies.

Jol managed Spurs a few years ago. I personally don't rate him much, but he's our manager now, so I wish him all the best.

It's again sliding doors on Stevenage Road. Nine new faces will wear the beloved white shirt, with winger Bryan Ruiz, a Costa Rica international, the shiny signing at over £10m from Dutch top-flight side Twente. Then Fulham make business in my country as former Liverpool left-back John Arne Riise comes in from Roma, Czech international defender Zdeněk Grygera is signed from Juventus and Swiss talent Pajtim Kasami joins from Palermo.

It's with a heavy heart that we see the icon Zoltán Gera going back to West Brom on a free. Paintsil moves to Leicester after his many unforgettable rounds of appreciation at Craven

Cottage. Dikgacoi and Greening also go to Palace and Forest respectively. Salcido goes back home after never really impressing down the left.

I'm now working in Formentera, the beautiful island in the middle of the Mediterranean Sea. Before accepting the offer, I make sure the bar I'll work in is fully equipped with Sky Sports.

And the answer is yes. Cool, I can watch Premier League games. The first six Fulham ones, though, are matches that can be missed.

Four points out of a possible 18 is a horrific start of the season. The opening-day 0-0 draw versus Aston Villa is a clear sign of things to come and is followed by the Whites being beaten 2-0 at Wolves and 2-1 at Newcastle, Dempsey opening his account. Then there are two home draws in a row, 1-1 with Blackburn and 2-2 with Manchester City, although in the latter case at least we came back from two goals down. September ends with another poor performance, 0-0 away at West Brom.

For the second season running, a poor start of the campaign sees us just above the relegation zone on goal difference. The team is yet to gel and our attack seems to rely too much on individual efforts from Demps or Zamora, when fit.

Next to come is the home derby against QPR, which – with Chelsea – is one of the games we supporters look for when the calendar is revealed.

It's a magic and unexpected performance in which, all of a sudden, everything seems to work as we record a 6-0 thumping and Craven Cottage goes wild! I recall watching it with a couple of friends, the working season almost over and only us in the bar, enjoying a good homemade burger and beers.

Neil Warnock's QPR are torn apart by a wonderful Fulham display with Andy Johnson bagging a hat-trick, Murphy converting a penalty, and Dempsey and Zamora again on target.

Glory day, and Jol's machine is suddenly working. We're on the right path. Wrong. The last ten minutes then condemn us to a 2-0 defeat in Stoke, and more late goals send us to a 3-1 home loss to Everton. Louis Saha again scores against us after Ruiz's first Premier League goal for the club has levelled the match.

There are definitely problems which Jol is not assessing at present. Too many players are not in form yet.

I watched both games; the first one in Formentera and the second in Barcelona where I made a quick trip to see some friends and so I also took the chance to eventually visit the famous Camp Nou. Through a friend I managed to get a ticket for Barcelona–Sevilla. It smells goals.

Barcelona's iconic home ground is huge but inside it's not the best option for watching. If you're in the upper tiers, in fact, you might need a telescope to see the action properly.

I'm by the middle flank, so not so bad, and I'm quite young and my sight is perfect, but the goals are far away.

Incredibly, it ends 0-0 with even Messi failing to convert a penalty with the very last kick of a match I have to follow in the fog of a giant cigar being smoked by the not-so-gentle Catalan in front of me.

Back to Fulham matters and our best players, Dempsey and Dembélé, rescue a much-needed 2-0 win at Wigan. My birthday is approaching. Coincidence?

Jol's former club, Spurs, raid the Cottage with a 3-1 win a week later, and 25,000 people leave in panic. I'm one of them, I'm usually a good omen for my beloved Fulham but today it didn't work. I was so happy to be in London again just a few months after my May trip and I've also never liked Spurs, as you know.

Two other draws follow, 0-0 at Sunderland and a good 1-1 at Arsenal, conceding again in the last ten minutes.

Clint Dempsey thankfully must have something against Liverpool because once again his goal gives us three vital points and opens a month of December where Fulham collect two wins, two draws and two defeats.

The Whites beat potential relegation rivals Bolton 2-0, Dempsey scoring again; they lose 2-0 in Swansea and are smashed 5-0 by a rampant Manchester United at Craven Cottage where the Red Devils have five different scorers.

The last two games of the month see us drawing both 1-1, a nice Christmas gift on Boxing Day at Stamford Bridge and another victory disappointingly eludes us at Norwich when they equalise in the 94th minute. Orlando Sá had previously put us in front. I still have clear pictures of when he let fly from outside the box. It's his only goal in our colours.

At the turn of the year, Fulham sit 14th on 23 points. Bolton, with 16, are 18th.

I spend New Year's Eve in Milan with my new girlfriend Elisa looking for a flat to rent as we'll be both working there in 2012, but I'm back home in time to watch Fulham's victory over Arsenal. What a game; 1-0 down until the time of the game we usually concede, then Sidwell in the 85th and Zamora in the 92nd win it for us and a packed Cottage erupts.

Twelve days go by and it seems it's enough for our guys to forget about the great win in the derby. Blackburn Rovers give Jol's men a lesson, winning 3-1, but thankfully if we go down then we quickly get up, our Whites tearing Newcastle apart 5-2 in London. Honour restored. Demps pockets a hat-trick; Murphy and Zamora convert penalties. After a performance like this, it's then a real pity we get held, again at home, by West Brom.

February begins with a nightmare in Manchester and another football lesson by City with a 3-0 defeat and no excuses.

So here I am in Milan with my girlfriend and her dog and of course the satellite dish! Thankfully Elisa is okay with football and sometimes she even watches the games with me. It's pizza and beer night, I'm screaming, cursing and acting, she's laughing at me but supportive enough if we lose and celebrating when we do well.

On 11 February, Fulham welcome the usually irksome Stoke City, but our new signing, Russian striker Pavel Pogrebnyak, scores his first goal for us. Our classic 2-1 win is back and three points are in the bag. And the Pog takes just seven minutes to cement a place in our hearts when, a week later, he finds the net again, winning the Loftus Road derby 1-0 and the double over QPR is sealed.

'Feed the Pog and he will score' is now the chant in fashion and it seems the guy is really hungry for goals. A 5-0 thumping of Wolverhampton Wanderers has again his name all over with three goals for the Russian beast, two by Clint and another good win in the day.

So when the goals stop for three weeks in a row, we're all baffled. Weimann wins it for Villa in the 92nd minute and rampant Swansea then come away from Craven Cottage with a 3-0 win. Nine days later Fulham lose, almost as usual, at Old Trafford, Rooney with the only goal.

Three games, three defeats, no goals.

March, the month opened with a 5-0 win, is eventually wrapped up with another home victory, 2-1 over Norwich thanks to two early goals by the ever-present Dempsey and Duff. Two goals I celebrated live! I love being here at Craven Cottage, I feel alive and I sing, always, out and loud.

Dempsey is in the scoring form of his life and he gets another brace when the Whites raid Bolton. Another new signing, former Real Madrid midfielder Mahamadou Diarra, completes the 3-0 rout.

I watch these games back home in Vicenza as my dad is really sick and so my departure for Formentera has been delayed. It's really strange to see your old man, a retired builder, lying on a bed, unable to complete basic tasks. My mum is distressed and tired after almost three years assisting him. They've been married for over 50 years and she's as devoted as ever.

Just two days after the exploits in Bolton, Fulham get a deserved home draw against our other neighbours, Chelsea. And it's seven points in three when they hit Wigan with the classic 2-1. Pog is back on the score sheet and Senderos heads in the winner after Boyce had put the struggling Latics one up.

A double encounter in Merseyside then awaits. Goodison Park is again shy of happiness for us, Everton shutting down the Whites with a tremendous 4-0 home win, but it's the rare glory in Anfield that counts more for me. Skrtel's fifth-minute own goal is enough to bring a famous victory back to London.

Our superheroes salute the Cottage in the right way, disposing of Sunderland with our signature 2-1 win thanks to Dempsey marking his 17th league goal and Dembélé getting the winner.

Unfortunately Jol's former club beat him again and Fulham end the season with a defeat at White Hart Lane.

Overall it's been another great campaign for the Whites, ending up in ninth place, level on points with Liverpool, who qualify for the Europa League thanks to their better goal difference. Fulham have recorded 52 points, 14 wins, ten draws and 14 defeats.

I must admit that I'm surprised. As I said previously, I'm not a great fan of Martin Jol, but you have to give him credit for what we've achieved this season, establishing Fulham as a tough team to face and a top-ten finish for the second year running – the third time in four years.

The only disappointment was a group-stage exit from the Europa League. Fulham had qualified again, this time through the fair-play rule, and easily got past Faroe Islands minnows Runavík.

Our Cottagers then easily disposed of Irish side Crusaders, 7-1 on aggregate with even Matthew Briggs scoring a goal. He's a guy who really looked promising and he got some chances, did well, so I thought he could break in more often and maybe come good. He always looked a genuine boy so it's a pity it never properly worked out.

Fulham qualified for the play-offs by beating Croatians RNK Split 2-0 at the Cottage after another 0-0 away draw.

Dnipro, a tricky Ukrainian opponent, were then well beaten 3-0 in London with Dempsey bagging his first double of the year. Fulham then lost 1-0 away but qualified 3-1 on aggregate.

It was Europa League again for Fulham just two years after our run to the final. Dutch side Twente, Poland's Wisła Kraków and Odense of Denmark were our opponents.

The first two games made us believe in a repeat of the miracle, drawing 1-1 at home with Twente followed by a good, neat, 2-0 win in Denmark with Johnson scoring all our goals.

Dembélé's red card proved pivotal in the narrow defeat in Poland towards the end of October, a defeat soon overturned as a birthday gift to me on 3 November with a 4-1 football lesson and Johnson scoring another brace against Kraków.

The 89th-minute 1-0 defeat in the Netherlands on the first day of December slightly complicated our life but welcoming bottom team Odense for the last game of the group gave hope for progress.

Incredibly, and sorry about this, so Fulhamish, our boys managed to draw the game 2-2 in front of 15,000 open-mouthed fans. Dempsey and little wizard Frei seemed to have put the game to bed in the first half as we led 2-0 inside 31 minutes.

Andreasen got one back for Odense on the 64th minute. The Danish had nothing to play for and were already mathematically eliminated. Our team probably relaxed too much and in the 93rd minute the unthinkable happened. Fall headed in the equaliser after Orlando Sá had just missed a clear chance to put the game to bed.

In Poland, Wisła Kraków's supporters were going bonkers after their team had beaten Twente 2-1 and celebrated an unexpected qualification.

I was working and constantly checking the phone for updates, and with us 2-0 up I thought we had it and concentrated more on what I was doing, so just imagine how I reacted when I finally checked again. I was so relaxed and happy that I almost fainted when I saw how it ended. I couldn't believe it; my colleagues were asking if everything was okay.

It could have been great again, because history repeating is not so uncommon. Atlético Madrid, in fact, won that edition.

One of Us

Soundtrack: 'A Kind of Magic' – Queen

A SOLID and respected side is how to look at Fulham in 2012. Martin Jol is in the driving seat and we look on the up.

I eventually get to Formentera at the beginning of June. My dad is really bad so I'm expecting the worst but I could not delay my departure any longer as work is calling.

If only I had known my girlfriend, who was already on the island, would leave me almost the day after I got there, and that my colleague and friend would reveal himself as the careerist I feared he was, at my expense, I could have stayed longer at home helping out.

Life goes on anyway and I live mine while keeping a good relationship anyway with my former girlfriend, which I don't do with the guy. I leave my former job and start working in the new place but only two days after I have to fly home as Dad passed away.

It's sad but at least he's no longer suffering. He never liked football, and most of the time he was not even watching important Italy games. He also didn't like me playing it but from time to time when I was taking a corner I could see him hidden behind some other spectators.

Fulham's transfer market this time is much thinner than usual. Mladen Petrić, who scored that marvellous free kick against us in the Europa League semi-final, signs on a free from Hamburg. Wigan's Colombian striker Hugo Rodallega also joins as a free agent.

On the last day we also get former Manchester United winger Kieran Richardson from Sunderland for £2m, the same amount required to sign Iran international midfielder Ashkan Dejagah from Wolfsburg. Two of the three new players in have come from the two German teams we beat on the way to the Europa League Final. Defender Sascha Riether also signs from 1. FC Köln.

Fireworks are then mixed with surprise when it's announced that Manchester United star Dimitar Berbatov has just signed for Fulham! I have to read the news twice because at first I thought they wrongly put us in that sentence.

But it's real. Berbatov signs for us for £5m while Juventus and, most of all, Fiorentina, are left fuming.

I personally think this signing is the perfect example of how highly Fulham are now regarded. It's something that simply feels like a dream.

Berbatov is sensational; he showed the world with Tottenham first and later at United that he's class. Some call him lazy but I reckon that everybody has their own skills. You can't ask Berbatov to press defenders all over; he's a proper number nine, an attacker, a central striker. His role is scoring goals and he does it, so let him do that and somebody else can run after the ball or opponents' heels.

As happy and over the moon as I am about it, I'm as sad at seeing Andy Johnson and Danny Murphy leave, both on a free. It's like deleting two faces from a family portrait. Pogrebnyak is lured to Reading, Etuhu is sold to Blackburn.

Moussa Dembélé goes to Spurs for £15m, great business and a great player who leaves. I'm also troubled when my beloved Clint Dempsey follows Dembélé to White Hart Lane.

He wanted to play at the highest level and fight for trophies so I can't blame him too much. I simply hoped Al-Fayed would spend big and make us a force in the Premier League able to keep its best players but it's not so.

It's with wet eyes that I think back about that magic lob against Juventus and all of Dempsey's goals and class. He was and still is my favourite Fulham player of all time, and one of my top ten ever.

I personally think these departures – all players who aren't replaced – are the perfect example of how low Fulham's ambitions are at present. Was Mark Hughes right? Only the future will tell.

After the usual summer friendlies, where youngsters like my countryman Marcelo Trotta, plus northern boys Lauri Della Valle and Alexander Kačaniklić, have a go, Fulham start their 12th consecutive top-flight campaign, destroying Norwich 5-0 with our new number ten Petrić bagging a brace. But if we scored five in one we then concede six in two. A narrow 3-2 defeat by Manchester United is followed by a 3-0 thumping by West Ham in east London.

Thankfully, confidence and faith are soon restored with two wins in a row, the Whites recording a 3-0 home victory over West Brom with Berbatov scoring two, and following that up with a 2-1 at Wigan where, as usual, a player – this time Rodallega – scores against his former team.

September ends in defeat, 2-1 at home to Manchester City. Petrić puts us in front but the incredible pair of Agüero and Džeko win it for the Cityzens.

Six games in, three wins and three defeats. Consistency is not a word in Fulham's vocabulary. Thankfully even boredom isn't there.

October goes by undefeated, a 1-0 home win over Villa coming in between two goal-rich draws. In both of those, we go in front in the 88th minute – at Southampton and Reading – only to then concede an equaliser even later.

Martin Jol's Fulham play open, free-flowing football where scoring a goal more than the opponents seems to be the aim. I'm okay with it; I like entertaining football much more than a classic game between two Italian sides where, too often, the side that goes in front parks the bus just waiting for the right moment to counter-attack. If it works it's a 2-0 win, if it doesn't it will probably end 1-1 with both sides playing a risk-free game that will bore you to death.

Our Whites keep both the unbeaten run and the goal party going in the first two games of November. First is a 2-2 home draw with Everton; this time Sidwell, in good scoring form from the midfield, earns us a point in the 90th minute. Then it's pure entertainment in a 3-3 draw at the Emirates where Fulham first go down 2-0, then up 3-2 thanks to Berbatov's brace, only for Giroud's second to claim a point for the Gunners. It's a little surprising when Sunderland take the points at the Cottage a week later. Petrić is again on target for Fulham, who are unable to keep their scoring form in the away 1-0 defeat at the hands of Stoke.

I just said I don't like boring games and I prefer to lose 3-2 instead of a 0-0 draw. Stoke are one of those teams that play an almost entirely physical style which also drives me mad.

Football is a game so it should be entertaining; players should be good with their feet and not stocky giants overpowering others. I look for the great pass and the amazing skill. I want to see class not shoulder pushes, throw-ins turned into crosses, and long balls.

A rare clean sheet eventually comes in the 0-0 draw at Stamford Bridge on 28 November but just three days later Tottenham, again on the winning side against their former manager, hit us 3-0.

Fulham bounce back by beating Newcastle 2-1, Sidwell again on target and Rodallega with the winner. But once more two defeats await – a very annoying 2-1 loss at QPR with Taarabt looking like Maradona, and a 4-0 trashing received at Anfield with Skrtel making amends for last year's own goal.

The slump in form continues throughout December, making the 2012 Christmas time a period to forget. Berbatov scores early for us against Southampton, but Rickie Lambert's 85th-minute penalty sees us winless again. Even worse is the 2-1 home defeat by Swansea in the last game of the year when Ruiz's effort is not even enough for a point.

Seven points in 11 games is the poor return of November and December, so let's close this 2012 quickly and welcome the new year please.

In December my girlfriend and I take her parents to London but there's no live game for me so the year ends without visiting the Cottage or somewhere else to support the Whites. Part of this was due to my father's illness but I promise myself that won't happen any more.

Then 2013 begins with our 2-1 trademark result away to West Brom with Berby bagging one and young prospect Kačaniklić, who's getting more and more playing time under Jol, winning it for Fulham. Unfortunately our rollercoaster continues with an unimpressive 1-1 home draw with Wigan and a 2-0 defeat away to Manchester City. We close the month hammering the Hammers, pardon the pun, 3-1, with Berbatov again on the score sheet.

February has three games and we record all possible results. It starts with an unlucky 1-0 defeat at home to Manchester United, Rooney scoring in the 79th minute. A stalemate 0-0 draw in Norwich can be forgotten about, and the month ends with a 1-0 home win over Stoke. Berbatov's goal with the last kick of the first half provides a much-needed three points.

Incredibly, a long month like March has only two games. Fulham begin with a 2-2 entertaining draw at Sunderland, even if being two up and not leaving with three points is not fun. But a win then comes, 1-0 at White Hart Lane, again thanks to Berbatov's effort. The law of the former player scoring against his old club once again.

I'm in London in March but there's no chance to watch any game. It snows heavily and London is always so beautiful.

I meet up with Cristina, a friend I've always had a crush on. It was never the right moment even if I know she likes me too. We go out for dinner and then we have some drinks together. This time chemistry is unstoppable and we end up together at her place. She's stunning and when I leave we exchange a kiss that goes beyond words.

My only resource for games is Sky and it's on there that I watch our guys winning their second derby in a row as QPR leave Stevenage Road empty-handed. West London is white. Even the weather knows it. The thriller finishes 3-2. Berbatov scores twice and there's an own goal, before Taarabt scores in the 45th minute. The second period is nervy. Rémy, a future Chelsea man, scores early and then Sidwell is sent off with ten minutes to go, but luckily nothing more happens.

Our starting XI is peculiar with an incredible collection of ten different nations. If it wasn't for the two Norwegians, Hangeland and Riise, we would have fielded 11 players from 11 countries:

Schwarzer – Australia
Riether – Germany
Senderos – Switzerland
Hangeland – Norway

Riise – Norway
Sidwell – England
Karagounis – Greece
Dejagah – Iran
Ruiz – Costa Rica
Duff – Ireland
Berbatov – Bulgaria

Astonishing and, personally, quite awful. I've never been a fan of the effects of the Bosman law. Teams have been losing identity and national pride, and young talents are forgotten for the most exotic name. Mind you, it's not racism, nothing like that. I hate racism. Times change but I simply don't like this situation. My favourite era under these terms was the 1980s when in Italy, for example, a club could have a maximum of three foreign players in their ranks.

Anyway, that win over QPR on 1 April really fooled us as four defeats and a draw followed, leaving me speechless. Again.

Cissé scores in the 93rd minute in the 1-0 loss at Newcastle, although the 1-1 draw at Villa Park could have been okay if we didn't then get smashed 3-0 by Chelsea by the Thames, with David Luiz and John Terry bagging the goals between them.

And defenders seem to enjoy scoring against us as Arsenal centre-back Per Mertesacker gets the only goal in the 1-0 home defeat. We leave Goodison Park beaten by the same score and in April 2013 we have taken four points from six games.

We're well beaten in the first two fixtures of May too. Reading score four times to our two in reply at the Cottage, Ruiz's brace made useless, then Berbatov puts us in front the following week at home to Liverpool only for Sturridge's hat-trick to make it 3-1 to the Reds.

After five defeats in a row a final-day 3-0 away win at Swansea doesn't really take away the bitter taste, although

Berbatov scores his 15th league goal of the season. Fulham finish 12th and I find myself wondering what it could have been without this tremendous late record of six defeats in eight.

Cup-wise, Sheffield Wednesday knocked us out in the second round of the League Cup and Manchester United thumped us in the fourth of the FA Cup.

So goodbye, 2012/13. A decent finish, too many ups and downs, a great show by our new striker. What the 2013/14 campaign will bring nobody knows, but now is holiday time.

Although not for me. Since the middle of April I've been in the Balearic Islands. I have some work in Ibiza before the short ferry trip to Formentera for the summer season. My nephew Manuel is with me and we've driven all the way together from Italy and of course we've watched the Whites.

Back Where I Belong

Soundtrack: 'Nothing Compares 2 U'
– Sinéad O'Connor

IBIZA IS fun and the good weather is even better in a quiet month like April. The first bar I enter displays a Liverpool scarf so I leave. By the end of May we're already in Formentera which has now become almost a second home for me after three years. I'm working in my friend's new venture, an eye-catching high-quality pizzeria where I'm the manager. Of course Sky Sports is up and running in our flat. Having my nephew, who just turned 20, is great. He's a true Fulham fan too by now and we've already talked about a trip to Craven Cottage in winter.

Before that, there's the 2013/14 season ready to start and the usual merry-go-round of the transfer market.

Sascha Riether, who did well on loan, signs permanently, while Venezuela international centre-back Fernando Amorebieta and Ghana international midfielder Derek Boateng join for free from Bilbao and Dnipro respectively.

Dutch keeper Maarten Stekelenburg joins from Roma and we also bring in former Chelsea and West Ham star Scott Parker from Spurs. He's the flashy signing of the campaign, followed in by former QPR winger Adel Taarabt and well-travelled striker Darren Bent, both August loans.

As usual there are some sad goodbyes to wave; Europa League runners-up Davies, Baird and Schwarzer all leave to pursue their targets elsewhere. Petrić, who unfortunately faded away after a promising first season, moves to West Ham on a free. Young goalkeeper Marcus Bettinelli goes out on loan.

The biggest talking point is not the transfer market for once, it's the change in ownership. Fan favourite, beloved, at-times-grumpy Mohamed Al-Fayed, who's been selling most of his London assets, cedes Fulham FC to Pakistan-born American eccentric billionaire and tycoon Shahid Khan.

The moustached businessman made a fortune in automotives and already owns NFL franchise Jacksonville Jaguars.

As per the Martin Jol appointment, I'm sceptical. I don't know why but it doesn't give me goosebumps. Mo had seemingly lost interest, rumours say due to his legal battle following the loss of his son Dodi in 1997. But he still cared for Fulham so I'm a bit torn. If he sold to Mr Khan it probably means Mo reckons he's the right man to take the club further, but still, I'm not fully convinced. As usual though, I'll stick with the decision and will be behind the boys as loyal as ever.

Our pre-season tour destination is Costa Rica where Fulham play some easy local teams, with some tougher opponents awaiting for the other three friendlies. We end winless against Werder Bremen, Betis and Parma.

August is finally here and the Whites win at Sunderland thanks to Kasami's goal. Then we only gather one point in five games. Arsenal run riot by the river, winning 3-1 with Bent scoring the consolation goal. Ben Arfa's 86th-minute effort punishes us in the 1-0 away defeat at Newcastle. McAuley's 92nd-minute equaliser deprives us of the first home win in the 1-1 draw versus West Brom. Chelsea beat us 2-0 at Stamford Bridge and even Cardiff come away with three points from the Cottage, again thanks to a 92nd-minute winner.

By the end of September we're already struggling and we've also lost the interesting little tricky Turkish winger Karim Frei, who went back home to join Beşiktaş. My nephew Manuel and I hardly believe what we see and it's a pity that such an amazing summer is not continuing into the season.

October sees a rise in fortunes though and the Whites record two straight wins. Bent's strike is enough to give us our first home win in the 1-0 defeat of Stoke and then we destroy Crystal Palace at Selhurst Park with Kasami and Sidwell both scoring crackers which will be long remembered by fans and are contenders for the Goal of the Season award. Berbatov also opens his account and even Senderos goes on the score sheet. Happy days, finally.

But six defeats in a row hit us so hard it will be really difficult to come back up. Southampton only need the first half to win 2-0, while the following week Manchester United have virtually wrapped up their 3-1 win in the same amount of time. Much worse is our return to Anfield with Liverpool thrashing us 4-0, again after a horror first-half display in which we concede three goals. People are back at taking the piss out of my love for Fulham, which annoys me a little, but in the end I simply don't care.

November is an awful month during which we lose at home 2-1 to Swansea and we are well beaten 3-0 at Upton Park with two goals conceded in the last eight minutes. The situation is dramatic and nightmares of the past are knocking at the door of Stevenage Road. It looks to me that Jol's toy got broken, as we used to say in Italy.

Anyway, back from Formentera by the middle of October with Manuel and his younger brother Nicola, we've already booked our flights for 6 December.

I'm really looking forward to a trip together with my beloved nephews. Now they have grown up I really enjoy spending my time with them. Manuel is 20 while Nicola is 16. They'll fly on their own for the very first time and I'll meet them in Stansted. They're as buzzing as I am.

So finally the day has come and I'm here among thousands of travellers waiting for them. When I can see their faces, they're all smiles and we're quickly on our way to London. We'll stay at Ben's, a good friend of mine who I met in Formentera; he offered to host us in his house in Greenwich.

We're going to see Fulham's Sunday game versus Villa. Funnily enough my first game was with Villa and now it's going to be the same for Manuel. My nephews are hungry for football so on Saturday we try our luck and go to Crystal Palace where they play Cardiff.

Out of the train station, we jump in a taxi and at Selhurst Park we manage to get tickets. We've always respected Palace and especially their supporters who are quite loud again as expected.

We're in the Arthur Wait Stand and it reminds me a little like our own Johnny Haynes Stand. Architect Archibald Leitch designed both stadiums so that's no surprise. The Main Stand is impressive and the atmosphere is honestly great. Tony Pulis has just taken over so I don't expect a great amount of entertaining football. The Eagles dominate though and win 2-0, which we like, as none of us ever liked Cardiff and their style either.

In the end it was really a nice day out and we all loved Selhurst Park.

Let's not forget our main aim anyway: we're in London for our beloved Fulham who desperately need support. Palace got our sympathy but we're Fulham so bring on Aston Villa.

Beforehand we meet up with my dear friends Jeff, Mark and Ben, who I haven't seen for a couple of years now. Our meeting point is the Railway in Putney, a Wetherspoon pub with good ale at honest prices, packed with Fulham's supporters of all ages, who have been coming here for a long time before and after games.

I simply love this: the old bloke in his plain scarf together with his son or his nephew in their brand new shirt.

We have some beers and then walk towards Craven Cottage, with a little stop by the bridge where there's the best stand if you're looking for proper tasty and succulent British sausages. With a happy stomach we eventually move on and enter Bishops Park through the big gate. I've explained to my friends that this is my lucky ritual – in from the big gate, out from the small one. They laugh but they all follow me.

As usual I buy my match programme that will go straight into my collection, then we queue by the Hammersmith End turnstiles and we're in. I've missed this. There's nothing more to say. I simply feel at home here; alive, happy, ecstatic.

Martin Jol was dismissed after a run of seven consecutive losses and interim boss René Meulensteen, Sir Alex Ferguson's former assistant at Manchester United, will guide the boys today.

Our starting XI is Stekelenburg, Riether, Senderos, Hughes, Riise, Parker, Sidwell, Karagounis, Dejagah, Kačaniklić, Berbatov. Aston Villa, so far, have only lost once away from home.

But WE ARE FULHAM and with Parker dictating the rhythm and Berbatov displaying his class, we dominate Villa and half-time is like a bell saving a boxer from a knockout blow. We lead 2-0 thanks to Sidwell's effort and Berby's coolly taken penalty.

The second half sees a Villa penalty appeal waved away and the game ends in victory for the Whites. The Hammersmith End is all hugs and smiles. My nephews are so happy and so am I. This is what we came for and we couldn't be more satisfied.

We stay there taking in the good vibes; it's so nice to see the players feeling great again and all supporters being proud of them.

Hopefully it will be a turning point in a season so far very lacking in satisfaction for the whole club.

We take a picture to remember the day and the promise of repeating the feat is already in place. 'Actually we should schedule it as a yearly appointment at least' is our common agreement.

We love you Fulham.

Manuel gets the home kit with Berbatov 9 on the back. Wise boy. Three points in the bag, mission completed, see you soon.

That's All Folks

Soundtrack: 'An End Has a Start' – Editors

THE LUCK we brought is short-lived as not even a week after the home win over Villa the Whites get smashed 4-1 by Everton on Merseyside. Berbatov had levelled in the 67th minute with another cool penalty but then we conceded three times in 17 minutes. Manchester City punish us at the Cottage with a 4-2 scoreline in a game we manage to level 2-2 just to let two more in the 78th and 83rd minutes.

The Christmas gift is the return of Clint Dempsey on loan from Spurs. Of course I'm happy but I see it as a panic move and an attempt to revive the good times gone.

Boxing Day presents us with a misleading away result at Carrow Road where we dust off our signature 2-1 win for the occasion. We concede early but then Kasami levels and this timeit is our turn to score late, Scotty Parker winning it in the 87th minute.

The unthinkable is unfortunately just around the corner. Hull City, just four points above the relegation zone, thrash us 6-0 with a second-half performance that instead will long live in our worst nightmares.

In just four months we have fallen back to the muddy soil we were in six years ago, which is a long enough span to forget something so bad, so this hurts even more.

What's worse is that every time we seem to touch the bottom, we then manage to get something to give us hope again. And I really don't know if we can manage another great escape. Not this time, no.

Anyway, I keep the faith and I convince myself we can still make it. I hate being away though.

In the classic game on the first day of the year, the boys show again some pride and beat West Ham 2-1 after going one down early again. Sidwell, probably our MVP so far, scores again as does Berbatov.

New hopes, new smiles, new resolutions, all made useless by the four defeats in a row that follow.

Sunderland punish us at the Cottage with a sound 4-1 after Sidwell had levelled the match. Our beloved ground on the shores of the Thames is back to the dark days when almost everybody is running riot at our own expense.

A Santi Cazorla brace defeats us at Arsenal and ten days later Swansea beat us once more with even Berbatov scoring an own goal. These are signs which really scare me.

This is Berbatov's last appearance for Fulham as on the final day of the winter transfer window he joins Monaco on loan. I'm no one to judge but I see it as somebody who has seen how it's going and hasn't got the will, or the balls, to fight for the cause. I thought he could be our leader, instead he leaves. No problem, but all my respect is gone, dear Dimitar.

A couple of weeks earlier, inconsistent talent Ruiz had returned to the Dutch Eredivisie, this time to PSV Eindhoven.

We lose two defenders too as Senderos, a talent who never really reached his level, joins Valencia while our beloved Aaron Hughes makes the short trip to Loftus Road to join QPR.

We do have four new faces coming in. Youngsters Ryan Tunnicliffe and Larnell Cole join from Manchester United, Dutch international John Heitinga makes up for the departures at the back and at the very last moment we pull out the signing which should solve our problems up front as Greek international forward Kostas Mitroglou is ours for £11m. I follow football, I've heard of him, I've seen him playing a few times and he's good when not injured. And when we buy him, he's not fully fit.

January is gone; I'm back home with my mum who's slowly recovering from my dad's departure and the previous exhausting years at his helm. She's talking a lot again, a good thing, and all her memories of a child from the World War II years flood in. I decide to gather them all and my first book comes to life.

Fulham don't and are again beaten at home, 3-0 by Southampton with their striking partnership of Rodriguez and Lambert enjoying their day against us.

Surprisingly enough we then draw 2-2 at Old Trafford. A laudable Sidwell puts us unexpectedly in front, van Persie and Carrick score twice in three minutes to make the score 2-1 with ten to go, but Darren Bent, a ghost until now, sneaks a point in the 94th.

Three days later comes the home encounter with Liverpool. In the past few years we've been giving them a hard time and often got something out of these games so I'm still kind of hopeful.

We start well and Kolo Touré scores an own goal. Daniel Sturridge, another one who loves playing us, levels just before half-time. Little Brazilian wizard Philippe Coutinho then puts the Reds on top but shortly afterwards Richardson makes it 2-2. It's a thrilling game and I reckon several of us sense that we could do it.

Steven Gerrard has other ideas, however, and again we concede late to lose 3-2. It's already the fifth defeat since the turn of the year.

The Khan family decides on the second managerial change of the season, which is never a good sign. Felix Magath, who won the European Cup as a player and led Wolfsburg to a surprising Bundesliga title in 2009, is appointed on 14 February 2014. It's Valentine's Day. Is it the beginning of a love story? Only time will tell.

Magath's first game in charge at least doesn't end in defeat but doesn't change things much. A 1-1 draw at West Brom sees the hosts taking the three points away from us in the 86th minute.

The first two games of March are just another nightmare; we lose them both 3-1. The first one at home to arch-rivals Chelsea sees André Schürrle scoring a hat-trick. Then Cardiff take their own revenge after all the bad things I've said against them. Steven Caulker, a centre-back, scores a brace, but Lewis Holtby, another of our new faces, gets one back. His countryman Riether, one of the few with Sidwell to show some respect for the colours during this anonymous season, scores an own goal which definitely ends the contest.

Ashkan Dejagah scores the only goal in our first home win since 1 January, 1-0 over Newcastle. But that is quickly followed by two heavy thrashings – 5-0 at the Etihad with Yaya Touré grabbing a hat-trick, and 3-1 at home to Everton with Dejagah again on the score sheet only for Mirallas and Naismith to win it for the Toffees on the 79th and 87th minutes. Our path is clear and we're going to be relegated. Even a die-hard like me now has no hope. My nephews are also devastated.

But we win twice in a row in the first two games of April. Firstly we do the double over Villa, coming away victorious from Birmingham with a 2-1 victory and this time the late goal is in our favour with Rodallega scoring in the 86th minute. Then we beat Norwich 1-0 at the Cottage with Rodallega scoring for the second game running.

I was there.

This time I took my friend Manuele to see the boys in white. I had to go to my former office to talk to my friend and former manager Antonio for some work I could do online from Italy, so I picked the weekend when Fulham were at home. A no-brainer!

And it's the Railway and lucky gates, for which my mates Jeff and Mark still tease me, but in the end they again follow me in this typical Italian superstitious ritual.

It seems to work out pretty well.

And there's also time for a pint with the one and only Mr Cook!

There are still 12 points to go for. Okay, let's wear the armour once more and get behind the boys even from a long distance.

The first of four finals is at White Hart Lane and statistics are against us. Spurs come out on top, winning 3-1, even though Sidwell had levelled it for us immediately after Paulinho's opening goal.

With three games left the table is:

TEAM	GAMES PLAYED	POINTS
West Ham Utd	35	37
Swansea City	35	36
Hull City	34	36
Aston Villa	34	35
West Bromwich Albion	33	33
Norwich City	35	32
Cardiff City	35	30
Fulham	35	30
Sunderland	34	29

The one that really counts is the following week though, when Fulham host Hull in a survival battle at a fully booked Craven Cottage.

And the first chance is wasted when the Whites again concede a late goal after turning the initial disadvantage upside down. Nikica Jelavić, who had already scored against us when playing for Everton, puts the visitors in front after 20 minutes. In the second half Fulham show character as Dejagah and Amorebieta score two goals in three minutes. Our old ground is again rocking and belief is growing. But Shane Long has other ideas and with just three minutes to go he breaks our hearts, sending the Tigers' bench into mayhem. It finishes 2-2, leaving us all speechless. And probably hopeless too.

Hull are safe on 37 points with just two games left, confirming their Premier League place for next year.

Cardiff lost and are now bottom with 30 points, while Sunderland won and are up to 32, just above defeated Norwich who stay at 32 but trail on goal difference. Villa lost and remain on 35, while West Brom won one and lost one and are now on 36.

We travel to the unfavourable Britannia Stadium at the same time as Villa and Hull face each other in the Midlands while Sunderland visit Old Trafford. West Brom and Norwich face the toughest games at Arsenal and Chelsea respectively.

Stoke are tenth with 44 points so they've got nothing to play for on paper, but this is not Italy. Sorry for being so critical of my home country but facts talk quite clearly. Too often, teams already safe don't play at their best in the last few games of the season, which is really ugly and unsportsmanlike, in my opinion.

And unfortunately for us the Potters really play as if it was a cup final, winning 4-1 with Fulham probably crumbling under the pressure.

After another painful performance, the Whites remain second from bottom and relegation is confirmed. We say goodbye to the Premier League after 13 seasons.

The final game is a 2-2 draw with Crystal Palace at Craven Cottage, young Chris David scoring for us on the 94th minute to ensure we avoid defeat, for what it's worth.

We had already been eliminated from both cups in the fourth round but that really didn't matter. What matters is that we're down after an ignominious campaign in which we lost 24 games out of 38.

As always happens, there are many arguments about what went wrong and who made the mistakes. All I can say is that the club should have built on our European exploits and made us take the next step. That didn't materialise and now we're all here mourning and moaning.

It's going to be Championship again. The owners make it clear they want to bounce back immediately, funds will be available – and we continue with Magath in charge. What?! Even I know that the Championship is probably harder than the Premier League and that you need experienced coaching staff and players or otherwise you're in big trouble.

I breathe, deeply. Let's see what happens and hope for the best.

To the Rescue

Soundtrack: 'My Love for You Is Insane'
– Maximilian Hecker

WHEN YOU go down, the all-change bells ring out loud. Berbatov signs permanently with Monaco on a free and also moving on are Briggs, Heitinga, Riise, Duff, Etheridge, Sidwell, Boateng and even the iconic Brede Hangeland, who heads south to Crystal Palace. Karagounis and Diarra are released due to their heavy wages; Riether goes back to Germany while Richardson is sold to Villa. Kasami joins Olympiacos for £4.4m, and for a little more Dejagah goes to Al-Arabi. Goalkeeper David Stockdale joins Brighton. Brede's departure is probably the very final chapter of a tale to be long remembered in our hearts.

Stekelenburg accompanies Berba to Monaco and Mitroglou does the same with Kasami to Olympiacos, both on loan. At the beginning of September, Tunnicliffe and Kačaniklić move out on loan too.

All these players are replaced with Shaun Hutchinson, Tim Hoogland, Adil Chihi and Mark Fotheringham for free, together with pyjama-pant-wearing Hungarian goalkeeper Gábor Király. Money is spent on Adam Taggart, Kay Voser, Thomas Eisfeld and Nikolay Bodurov among others. All the hype is then reserved for the acquisition of the previous season's top Championship scorer and Scottish international Ross McCormack who comes in from Leeds United for more than £10m. From the Yorkshire club there's another striker joining in Matt Smith at £500,000.

Well, this is turning interesting and mouth-watering. Talented young left-back Kostas Stafylidis, a Greek international, also joins on loan from Bundesliga giants Bayer Leverkusen.

Summer friendlies are encouraging with our bright talents Cauley Woodrow and Moussa Dembélé – the same name but not the same player who had joined Spurs – looking like blossoming.

In 2014 I am again working in Milan as a maître d' of a five-star city centre hotel. I'm not a big fan of living in the City of Fashion as it's known, but for work it's a good spot.

The Championship is not shown regularly in Italy though so I've got to make up for that with internet access, but I'm really looking forward to an immediate return to the Premier League, even if that feels doubtful with this manager.

On 8 July I'm having lunch at home on my own. My flatmates are away so I decide to watch a movie and chill before getting ready for work. I pick *The Hangover Part III* and I don't know why but I feel kind of strange. There's just time for some laughs and I receive the message you'd never wish to. 'Simone, what happened?'

I don't understand. We exchange a couple more messages then Federico clears the air. 'Umberto.'

It's suddenly all confused and blurred. I kill the TV and tears come down as I start crying in a way I thought could only happen in the movies.

I jump in my car and drive back to Vicenza after explaining why to a very understanding hotel manager. I can honestly say the news hit me harder than when my brother called me to go home from Formentera saying my father passed away. We'll salute Umberto in proper fashion a few days later in his native town, celebrating him through the night in a way he'd definitely like. A few friends drinking and sharing great stories about our time with him.

I end up puking in a vase of flowers just outside the posh Cipriani Hotel on the Giudecca Island in Venice.

A few months later I'll get Umberto's face tattooed on my right arm. It's the best tattoo I've got.

The beginning of the season just confirms all my doubts about Fulham's setup. Seven defeats in the first eight outings is simply dreadful, especially when the only game without a loss is a draw.

We lose 2-1 at Ipswich Town then twice in a row at the Cottage, which, as a former Premier League team we should be making a fortress. Instead, it's 1-0 to Millwall and Wolves before getting soundly beaten 5-1 at Derby. The 1-1 home draw with Cardiff is only good because it's against another relegated club who are tipped for promotion. Three goals scored and none by our strikers. The embarrassment continues with a 3-0 routing by Reading and a 5-3 defeat at Forest. In this last fixture, at least, our attackers wake up. McCormack bags a brace and Rodallega gets his first of the campaign but we look absolutely out of our depth. At least Felix Magath is waved farewell to and replaced by former player Kit Symons. One of our own. Eventually.

I bet not many are sad about Magath going. His methods turned out being like those of a colonel in a military regime. His tactics have been bizarre and his medical ideas even worse. Hangeland recalled in an interview that the German gaffer ordered him to cure his physical problem with cheese. I'm open to different approaches rather than standard medicine but this was a step too far.

So let's forget about this madness and try to turn the page. The first game in charge sees Symons's Fulham losing again at home, 1-0 to Blackburn Rovers. That makes one point in nine games.

The new manager starts coming good by the end of September when we raid St Andrew's. Defender Hoogland scores his third in nine and Rodallega gets the winner. And then comes the long-awaited home win, a 4-0 thrashing of Bolton with Rodallega and incredibly Hoogland again on the score sheet. The following loss at Middlesbrough looks like a stumble because we promptly win at home to fellow relegated side Norwich, young Irishman Sean Kavanagh with the only goal. We look back on track!

A scintillating 3-3 draw at Rotherham follows, then three days later a 3-0 home hammering of Charlton with captain Scotty Parker getting the opening goal and Rodallega signing it off with a brace.

We absolutely are a totally different team – gelled, working, fighting. Two more goal-filled draws at the beginning of November keep us moving up the table. On my birthday we engage in a firecracker at Wigan, 3-3 with Ruiz, back from his loan, scoring a brace, including a last-gasp penalty to seal the point. Young Danish midfielder Lasse Vigen Christensen is beginning to make a name for himself in our ranks.

We then draw 2-2 at home to Blackpool, recovering after being 2-0 down and again Ruiz scoring the equaliser. In the third game in one week we overcome Huddersfield Town 3-1. Rodallega, Christensen with his second in three, and McCormack do the damage. We then lose the west London derby at Brentford and it's a painful one because Rodallega's effort seemed good value for the three points until the 81st minute. We promptly wake up though and come away with a win from Brighton, Darren Bent with the goal for the hosts against his old club but Rodallega and Christensen overturned it. That means a very respectable return of 21 points in 11 games.

One day at work I see a face I'm sure I know – Pajtim Kasami. I don't know what he's doing in Milan but that's his business, so I approach him and we talk about Fulham as I tell him I used to be a season ticket holder. He's a good guy and looks genuine when he says he was upset once we got relegated. He would have stayed but the deal Olympiacos offered to the club and himself was too good to refuse for both parties.

That's one of my last days in the job; different views with the caretaker manager make us think it's better for us to pursue different routes. I leave within two days to spend almost two months in Formentera, enjoying a week of holiday before being asked to help out in a friend's restaurant.

Summer is gone and autumn is time for planning, so I do bits and pieces back home and, in Milan, also go ahead with my book.

In the first week of December, Fulham get surprisingly smashed at the Cottage by Watford. Bettinelli's red card after just 18 minutes proves to be a wall too high to overcome.

Symons's men are made of a totally different material than under Magath and they show it once more. The Whites win away at the ever-difficult Leeds thanks to Rodallega's intervention, before beating Sheffield Wednesday 4-0. McCormack and Christensen are again among the scorers.

Parker and his team-mates end the year in a much undeserved manner by twice losing 2-0, at Bournemouth and at home to Brighton.

What a year 2014 has been. One of my best friends ever passing away a couple of weeks after we celebrated with a beer the news a bone marrow donor had been found. Fulham relegated from the Premier League after more than a decade.

When I eventually thought about giving Milan a chance and maybe establishing myself there, an old chap, disposed of by one of the city's top hotels, comes in and after promising me the moon work-wise, he pulls all his strings and gets me out of his way.

I must say I'm a bit tired of changing my plans due to other people. Maybe I should really focus on what I want rather than adjust to what life offers me.

Anyway, let's move on once more, there's not so long until February and my next trip to London and Fulham.

Vicenza vs Chelsea first leg poster

Piero and I at Barbarella

Rachel managed to capture the best photo ever: Del Piero just scored Italy's second goal against Germany

FFC letter inviting me to the game

Barclay's Premier League official confirmation letter

The jersey I won with my surname and the number 7, the week I'd won the competition in, later signed by a few players

FFC official invitation to the event

Picture of all weekly winners entering the final draw

My sister Marilena and my nephew Nicola at the home game v West Ham

Zamora and I at the club shop

My idol Dempsey and I

Umberto and I at Old Trafford

Umberto at the hospital   *Me and my new friends in Hamburg*

Mark showing up his FFC hairstyle   *Some Europa League match programmes*

Me and Sparky – Me and Hangeland   *Umberto trying to not get arrested*

The Cottage under the snow

My nephews Nicola and Manuel in the stands at Selhurst Park

Me and the boys finally together at Craven Cottage

Nicola with the Vicenza scarf – Manuel holding the Fulham v Juventus scarf

Mr Cook and my friend Manuele cheering with a pint

Atletico Madrid's trophy cabinet showing the EL Cup won beating Fulham

Proudly showing Mr Cook's birthday present

Fulham v Bolton programme

Martina, Davide and I by Es Trenc beach

Aaron, Nicola Z and my nephew Nicola by the Millwall graffiti

Giampaolo and I on a night out

Me with the NYC Marathon's medal under the Italian flag in Central Park

Showing off Cairney's jersey

Nicola Z. and my nephew Nicola moments after the beer incident

Me and the boys with the graffiti in Fulham Road

Seri taking a corner at Craven Cottage

Being a Fulham fan it's…your best life

The enormous fish and chips   *With the boys at The Rocket*

The very last drink at The Rocket   *Luca waking up in his*
Fulham shirt

My beloved Craven Cottage

Murphy's penalty against United

Zamora leaving the EL Cup behind

My first game at Craven Cottage. Fulham v Aston Villa

Dempsey scoring v Juventus

Championship play-off final win

Where the great escape effectively started

Gera scores v Hamburg

You Never Stop Learning

Soundtrack: 'Agony' – Unbelievable Truth

FULHAM LOSE their third game in a row when Cardiff beat us 1-0 in the very first Championship match of 2015 but like the phoenix they keep rising again. Kačaniklić, back from a loan, and Ruiz's 93rd-minute magic are enough to top former Whites striker Pogrebnyak's effort as Reading are disposed of 2-1 at the Cottage. Then comes another home victory, 3-2 over Nottingham Forest, with McCormack's 28-minute first-half hat-trick.

Blackburn beat us 2-1 at Ewood Park but the best time of the year has come and here I am back in the best city in the world. I simply love London. And I'm crazy about Fulham. Mario Balotelli, who we know through some connections and is now playing for Liverpool, promises my friend and me tickets for Anfield, but it seems that ground is cursed for me. He disappears and never gets back to us so there's no Merseyside again for me. Not that I worry about it, Craven Cottage is waiting and as always I'm glad and super happy to catch up with my mates Jeff, Mark and Ben who I've so much fun with.

It's time for the lucky gates again even if this time it's only a draw as Rodallega puts us in front after five minutes against Birmingham but David Cotterill levels in the 14th. And that's it, despite the early fireworks.

It's a point, and I'm okay with it; of course I hoped for a win but at least we move up in the table again.

A trip to London is also always a good excuse to see another dear friend, Mr Cook. At his house there's an empty room so here I am, even for just a couple of days, back where I lived for a few years.

Balham is always Balham. I feel so comfortable here; a coffee at Betty and Boo, a walk through Tooting Common.

Time goes by too fast when I'm in town and I'm already on my way back because I'm soon flying to Mallorca to explore the island for a business idea I have together with a friend.

Before that, we have a few hours to spend in Madrid waiting for the connection flight to the island so why not take the tube and pay a visit to the Vicente Calderón Stadium, home of Atlético Madrid?

And drop a little tear in front of their trophy cabinet.

The slip in form for Fulham becomes clear after losing 3-1 in Bolton and 2-1 at home to Ipswich, the Tractor Boys doing the double over us. The 0-0 draw in Millwall comes before getting badly beaten 3-0 at Wolves.

Bodurov and Woodrow score in the 2-0 home win over Derby, some revenge of the trashing suffered in the away game. Watford narrowly beat us 1-0 but we're again torn apart at home, 5-1 at the hands of Bournemouth.

A visit to Sheffield results in a 1-1 draw with Wednesday before Leeds claim revenge for our win over there. Stafylidis gets booked twice in two second-half minutes and the score is a clear 3-0 to them.

Nahki Wells shows up as Santa Claus in disguise when he misses two penalties allowing us to raid Huddersfield Town, 2-0. We're alive.

Or maybe not. Brentford beat us again, and it's a bad one – we suffer a 4-1 home defeat by our neighbours, another club doing the double over us. A talking point for our rivals. Our situation is now a little complex. While we looked play-off material not so long ago, we are now dangerously flirting with relegation again. And that would be disastrous.

Whatever happens next – if Symons and the boys have a clear-the-air chat, I don't know – definitely works. In five games we draw three times and win twice, amassing nine much-needed points. At Charlton we draw 1-1 then it's 2-2 at home to Wigan and 1-1 at Rotherham, with McCormack scoring three of the four goals. Then we win 1-0 at Blackpool thanks to Matt Smith's goal, and at the Cottage we beat Middlesbrough 4-3, denting their hopes of automatic promotion. We go 3-1 up, Middlesbrough make it 3-3 in the 88th minute, then we win it in the 94th. McCormack again scores a hat-trick with two second-half penalties included.

We follow that by losing 4-2 at Norwich to close a strange first season back in the Championship.

Fulham end up in 17th place with 52 points in 46 games, and an astonishing 22 defeats. Norwich are the only relegated team from the Premier League to bounce back immediately.

These three games are the first I watch from my new home, Palma, the capital of Mallorca. A great place where me and my business partner decided to start up our new venture. Once there we discover the Lennox pub which is in walking distance from our flat and shows all televised Championship games. It's not a cheap place but there's a good vibe and a decent pint of Guinness.

We spend the month of May redecorating a place we got for our bar on one of the numerous squares nearby the city centre. I'm super excited and very happy and proud I finally managed to realise my dream. Unfortunately all the good things go when my mate decides he's had enough and goes back to Italy. The place is on sale and my dreams are shattered.

The following months are tiring, especially psychologically, but thankfully my nephew Manuel is there with me as he came during the university break to help out. In those moments it's really good to have someone around.

When he leaves, Davide, my great friend since the time in the London hostel, comes to live on the island with his wife Martina. And that is really a life-saver.

Time goes on and Fulham prepare for another season in the Championship, again being tipped for promotion. I really like the new kit; it's classy with that black collar.

The transfer market once more brings in a load of new faces, this time mostly British. Maybe the management are learning from their mistakes. As I am.

Former Spurs star Jamie O'Hara signs on a free, US international defender Tim Ream joins from Bolton where he made a name for himself, and sprinter Ryan Fredericks, a right-back stolen from athletics, comes in from Bristol City. We also sign backup keeper Andy Lonergan, Ben Pringle, Jazz Richards from Swansea City but most of all, young talent Tom Cairney from Blackburn Rovers, a Scot who has successfully represented his nation at youth levels.

Loaned in are two young prospects at the back, Luke Garbutt from Everton and James Husband from Middlesbrough.

Tim Hoogland, one of the positives of the previous campaign, goes back to Germany; Hugo Rodallega has a good offer from Turkey and he also departs on a free. Bryan Ruiz goes for good and joins Sporting Lisbon, one of Portugal's giants.

Young talent Patrick Roberts is purchased by Manchester City for a hefty sum that aids our bank balance, and we also see a lot of fringe players leaving.

Some big names, or supposedly so, leave on loan: Stekelenburg to Southampton, Mitroglou to Benfica, Amorebieta to Middlesbrough.

Even our pre-season friendlies are of a higher level than the past and we do well, losing only once, narrowly, to Eintracht Frankfurt.

Our 2015/16 season begins in a bad way though, with two draws and two defeats in the opening four games. It's 1-1 with both Cardiff and Huddersfield, either side of 2-1 defeats to Brighton and Hull, the latter just relegated from the Premier League.

We end August with a 3-1 away win at Rotherham and then beat Blackburn 2-1 at the Cottage. Cairney, McCormack and Woodrow each have two goals to their names so far.

Sheffield Wednesday beat us 3-2 at Hillsborough and we're hammered for the first time this season, 3-0 by Wolves at Craven Cottage.

But in between there's a 4-0 thumping of arch-rivals QPR in yet another successful derby against them. Dembélé, Pringle and McCormack make it 3-0 by half-time, then McCormack scores again in the second half.

My private life and football are going along in a very similar way.

October arrives, the weather over here is amazing and a mild temperature accompanies us towards autumn.

Palma is the most visited place on earth with an estimated 20-plus million people coming to see its marvellous beauty. *The Times* also declares Palma as the best place to live in in the entire world. Wow.

I must say that it's a very beautiful city, with its cathedral majestically welcoming you from the airport. So far it has not been very nice to me, but only for my mistakes I must admit.

Fulham kick on. We all know how long and tiring is the Championship and October sees us playing five times in 27 days. And we end it unbeaten.

We draw 2-2 at Charlton and 0-0 at Middlesbrough. The third draw in a row is at home to Leeds. But by the end of the month the Whites are firing on all cylinders with a 4-2 home rout of Reading followed by a 4-1 victory at Bristol City. The strike partnership of Dembélé and McCormack steals the show with four and two goals respectively, bringing a much-needed nine points.

My birthday is a totally unexpected happy day which I celebrate the night before at the Gin Burger, the place I'm now working at as a barman, and the day after, on the beach, with some of the dearest people I have around me here.

The Kokomo is a bar right in Cala Major, one of my favourite beaches in Palma. Mr Cook makes the trip from London for this special occasion. It's my 40th birthday and his gift is also memorable.

Birthday celebrations are behind us and it seems as if Fulham's form is too with an unexpected reality check, Burnley beating us 3-1 at Turf Moor before a 5-2 home debacle to Birmingham City costs Symons his job. McCormack is still bagging goals but something is clearly not working properly so two caretaker managers take over, resulting in an even worse outcome.

Successive 1-1 draws at Milton Keynes Dons and at home to Preston end November. Forest show no mercy in their 3-0 thumping of a headless Fulham, who then draw again, this time 2-2 at home to Brentford before losing 2-1 to Ipswich at the Cottage. On 19 December comes another 2-2, this time at Bolton, ahead of another defeat, 2-0 at Derby. Four points in seven games is a return that is usually associated with a relegation-threatened team.

Eventually, on 27 December, Serbian former Chelsea midfielder Slaviša Jokanović is appointed and at least the year is closed well with a 4-1 beating of poor Rotherham.

A little cause for celebration for us fans.

Anyway, there's now a new manager in charge, someone whose reviews are very interesting, and his style of play is defined as 'possession-based attacking football'.

Fair enough. I am behind the lads and this new gaffer, who I remember in his playing days with Chelsea. Do well son and we'll pardon you for your past.

The Only Way Is Up

Soundtrack: 'Closing Time' – Semisonic

PERSONALLY, 2016 starts with ghosts from the recent past, gone but still in my memory, and some little scars in my heart. My dream is gone, almost all my money as well, but here I am, rebuilding my life. I'm still quite young so forward is the only way.

And Fulham's start to the new year is not helping. January is awful with one point in four games after losing 1-0 twice, at home to Sheffield Wednesday and Hull in the first and last games of the month. We lose 3-2 away to Wolves after being 2-0 down in 13 minutes and the only point comes from a 1-1 draw at Huddersfield. The situation in the table is definitely not good.

February brings some deserved joy at last with a 1-1 draw at Craven Cottage against Derby before we again beat QPR. Surely they won't face us for a while. At Loftus Road it's 3-1 for the boys in white with McCormack, Dembélé and Cairney all scoring in the last ten minutes of the first half. QPHahahahaha.

A 3-0 defeat at Blackburn is quickly forgotten about with a victory by the same score over Charlton, Cairney with a brace. We take a point at Leeds again thanks to Cairney before losing badly at home to Middlesbrough in a 2-0 scoreline. Dembélé and McCormack get us a point at Reading but we fall to defeat at home soon after, Burnley doing the double over us. Four days later, Bristol City beat us 2-1 in London through Tomlin's goal in the 90th minute.

What the hell is going on at Fulham?!

I'm working as manager at the Gin Burger. I'm always there and can't watch live games but I'm watching most at home on the internet before going to bed or whenever I can. Jokanović has definitely improved the quality of our approach. We play an attractive style of attacking football but we concede too many goals.

We're going to play another season in the Championship, which is a fact that really gets on my nerves.

Slav's ideas seem to kick in suddenly towards the end of the campaign when we take a good point in Birmingham with Rohan Ince scoring the only goal of his loan spell from Brighton and then, for the first time this season, three victories in a row come along, all by our trademark 2-1 score.

Beaten in London are the fake Dons, then Preston at Deepdale with McCormack and Dembélé each scoring in both games. We close the streak at Craven Cottage, Cardiff beaten by efforts from Parker and Hyndman, the latter in the 93rd minute.

Again comes the reality check. Brighton bring us fiercely back down to earth, beating us 5-0. Dembélé's 66th-minute goal looks enough to bounce back at Ipswich but Knudsen has other ideas and the 91st-minute equaliser is a slap in the face. We are then beaten 3-1 at home to Forest and 3-0 at Brentford, a result already sealed in a terrifying first half.

Fulham beat Bolton 1-0 in the last game of a season I'm here in London to salute and kick away. Cairney's solo effort is enough to put a smile on my face and bring some cheer to everyone gathered here despite the poor times.

Scotty's scream perfectly identifies our feelings.

A change somewhere is needed and I lead by example, leaving the Gin Burger crew to move into Bunker's Restaurant, a classy place with a casual approach where I actually had my very first meal in Palma back in February 2015.

Fulham stay up, but there's no happiness in that, finishing 20th in the Championship, 11 points above relegation, 23 from a play-off spot and a massive 38 points away from automatic promotion. It's definitely not good enough. Yes, we're well aware of how tough and exhausting this league can be. And we perfectly know how hard it is to get out of it, but wow, just avoiding relegation for the second year running is a bit too much even for a Fulham fan.

All we could do though is hope for the better in 2016/17, our third consecutive season in the Championship.

Slav is confirmed as manager and I like that a lot. Finally, after a few years of jokers, big egos and small results, I feel he's the right man to take us further and I like his style of play. He wants the ball to be passed around a lot and I reckon he follows Pep Guardiola's philosophy of 'as far as we've the ball, opponents don't'.

We're back at our in-and-out carousel as 11 players sign permanently plus three on loan for a staggering total of 14 new faces. And that's nothing compared to the 29 who leave Stevenage Road! Kevin McDonald comes in from Wolves, Norway captain Stefan Johansen joins from Scottish giants Celtic, and among the others coming in are Sone Aluko from Hull City, Austria international Michael Madl from Sturm Graz, Tomáš Kalas and Lucas Piazon from Chelsea, and Chris Martin from Derby.

As for the departures, former loanees Mitroglou and Stekelenburg are signed permanently by Benfica and Everton. Dan Burn goes to Wigan while Kačaniklić joins Nantes for free, and that's astonishing to me. Emerson Hyndman will be a Bournemouth player and Moussa Dembélé joins Celtic, so we'll get compensation for him.

Here I've got to stop a little and be annoying maybe but I really don't understand how we can let half of our striking force, a raw diamond in the making, go for very little. We've known for a while the length of his contract, he did well and probably caught the eyes of a bigger fish than us. Did we really try everything we could to keep him though?

Amorebieta goes back to Spain, this time with Sporting Gijón, while the board decide to take an offer from Aston Villa for McCormack who leaves for over £12m.

Defenders Denis Odoi and Ragnar Sigurðsson sign, with wide attackers Floyd Ayité and Neeskens Kebano, plus highly rated Spanish midfielder Jozabed and former Brentford keeper David Button to complete the list of permanent signings.

So 38 + 15 = 53 is the amount of goals we lose in just over a month by saying goodbye to McCormack and Dembélé. Our striking force, one of the best in the whole league, dismantled.

Pre-season is again encouraging. We play eight friendlies and only lose one, away to Real Betis, while we beat, among others, Spurs 1-0, Brighton 3-0, Preston 5-0 and Palace 3-1. Is this the right season to go up?

As work slows down a bit at the crowded and successful Bunker's Restaurant, I immediately check Fulham's opening-day score, and yes, we kick off on the right foot with a 1-0 win at home to Newcastle who just got relegated from the Premier League. Matt Smith scores the goal. A week later we beat again Preston North End, and this time it counts, adding three more points to the bag with Smith scoring for the second game running in a 2-1 win. Is he going to be our new McCormack?

Our good form continues and we finish a great month of August unbeaten, drawing 1-1 at Leeds and 2-2 at home with Cardiff, where Ryan Sessegnon, who has just turned 16, scores for us. We then beat Blackburn away thanks to Cairney's goal in injury time. It's his second goal in the last three games. Wow. I know it's too early to get excited but we really look good and 11 points out of a possible 15 is a very nice start.

Dreams are promptly cooled however as September is instead a winless month with two defeats, both at Craven Cottage. We lose 1-0 to Birmingham with Madl being sent off and then 4-0 to Bristol City, this time with Kevin McDonald seeing red.

In between are lacklustre draws with Burton – 1-1 with young Sessegnon again on the score sheet – and 0-0 at Wigan. The last game of the month is also a draw, this time 1-1 at Forest, where Cairney's effort seals the point.

And if you think that was bad, the first game of October is even worse. QPR avenge past poor results by beating us 2-1 at our own ground. It's a lunchtime thriller I unfortunately manage to watch live at the Shamrock pub. The first and last time I've betrayed my lucky Lennox, and I'm punished.

I'm puzzled. We were flying high and playing good football only a month ago and now we're struggling to get a goal and a point.

Everything changes with the trip to Barnsley where we're back to our best and win 4-2. Norwich go two up with two penalties at the Cottage three days later but Johansen and Martin manage to get us back on track for a point. We're then unlucky to come away empty-handed from Villa, Kodjia winning it in the 80th minute. Pity.

A sign we've already forgotten about September comes when we recover from it with a thumping 5-0 against Huddersfield Town. Martin scores two and Chelsea loanee Lucas Piazon gets his second in four games.

Mallorca is still blooming and booming with tourists. Summer has been wonderful, sunny, gorgeous. I really enjoy working here. We have a lot of foreign customers so I can keep my English working. Tips are good and we give out a high quality of food and service. With Luigi and Rudy, chef/owner and sous-chef, both being Italians, we get on well which always helps.

I'm also following a business academy and once a month I get to go to Italy with my mate Davide for the workshops.

My 41st birthday is properly celebrated with typical Mallorcan food and Fulham's gift is a 2-0 away win at Brentford with Aluko and Cairney scoring.

Jokanović likes to play with a 4-2-3-1 wide formation which often sees this starting XI:

Button

Fredericks; Kalas; Ream; Malone

McDonald; Johansen

Piazon; Cairney; Aluko

Martin

Odoi sometimes plays at right-back or centre-back, Matt Smith can replace Martin, and Sessegnon often lines up on the left.

With this victory we're up to seventh so just off the play-off spots. Yes it's still early but is better to be there than somewhere else.

Maybe it has got to our heads though and we draw one and lose the other of our remaining games in November. It finishes 1-1 against Sheffield Wednesday in London, Malone with a very late equaliser, and we're beaten 2-1 at Brighton after being one up thanks to McDonald.

We bounce back immediately by trashing Reading 5-0 at home, the second time we record this score this season, and we're on a scoring spree again when we draw 4-4 at Wolves. It's a proper rollercoaster. Wolves go two up, we overturn it

3-2 thanks to Johansen and Ayité with two goals in quick succession and then Cairney, Doherty makes it 3-3, Cavaleiro's goal means advantage Wolves, only for Ayité's second which sees the away end exploding in joy in the 94th minute.

We have got momentum and Rotherham are beaten 2-1 at Craven Cottage, Ayité in fine scoring form with the second after Johansen's opener.

We're up and running towards the end of the year, we draw 2-2 at home with Derby, then come away 2-0 winners from a difficult ground at Ipswich, defensive colossus Sigurðsson scoring the second.

We finish on a high as the Reading game, originally planned for 30 December, is postponed as the fog takes over.

New Year's Eve means working this time but it's fun with a set menu, a reduced amount of guests, celebrations at midnight and by 1.30am we're on the street going around the borough for the wishes to our friends and colleagues at other restaurants.

In the end, it's been a good year. I'm standing strong again, the past is the past and I've moved on. I've got work, no more debts, some very good friends around, and I'll never forget what Davide and Martina did for me. Fulham are playing well and up there fighting for promotion. And I've just spoken to my nephews planning for a weekend in London, probably in February, to watch our beloved Whites.

Ouch!

Soundtrack: 'Almost Happy' – K's Choice

WELCOME INTO 2017, from the beach! Martina, Davide and I drive to one of the best ones on the island, Es Trenc. We greet the new year and also spend some time together as they'll soon go back to Italy for good. They were simply amazing for what they did for me and they'll leave with Mallorca in their hearts so I'm at least happy for that.

Here comes the winter transfer market. Busy days for the owners, managers ringing their bosses asking for money to spend, unhappy players knocking at their manager's door looking for a way out, agents ringing their clients hoping to cash in on another double-figure move.

Lucas Piazon's successful first half of the season earns him an extension of his loan while Ivory Coast striker Gohi Cyriac and Greek midfielder Thanos Petsos are loaned in to replace Matt Smith. He did well for me, but he goes to QPR. Poor him.

Jozabed, who almost never featured for us, joins Celta Vigo until the end of the season. Promising young keeper Marek Rodak goes to Accrington to gain experience and I'm quite surprised once more when we let Christensen and Woodrow join Burton Albion.

The first game of the year is definitely not a good one as we lose 2-1 to Brighton, but a 12-day break helps and this time we win at home, 2-0 over Barnsley. The following two derbies are not so rewarding though. At Loftus Road, Martin, who had scored the previous game, misses an early penalty but luckily he then equalises later on and we take a point. He misses another penalty away at Reading, imitating our opponents, who do however manage to score one and win 1-0.

On 1 February we win on the road, 2-0 at Burton, confirming my doubts about LVC and Woodrow going there. Malone is enjoying a rare run of scoring form while Johansen instead continues his good one this campaign. We then lose a weird game in Birmingham, 1-0 to the hosts.

Next to come are two home games in four days, against Wigan and Nottingham Forest. And these are the games we're going to be there for.

My nephew Nicola, together with his mates Nicola and Aaron, will keep me company in London.

I found a place for them to stay not far from Putney Bridge station, I'll stay at Mr Cook's as I'm happy to go back to Balham even if just for a few days.

Unfortunately, the accommodation in Putney is not that good. It's a super-simple room with furniture even a discount shop would feel ashamed to sell. That's not a big deal though as the boys will only use the room to sleep at night, but the bathroom is a real disgrace where the only window has a broken pane. And it's February too. As we get in, a Spanish girl starts banging on the door. We exchange a few words, show her the booking and she goes quiet.

The boys don't care about it too much and we're all looking forward to the games. The first one is on at the classic time, Saturday at 3pm. We meet up in the Railway pub with Jeff, Mark and Ben. It's always so cool to see them, we have a great time and I love them. Jeff lives in Littlehampton and he makes the train trip every time. Fair play to him. We have a few pints, here they're quite cheap but really good. Doom Bar, Abbot, Spitfire and Hobgoblin are just a few of the ales you can enjoy in there. I like my beer. I grew up with the lager culture in Italy but since my days in London I moved on to the ales – more taste, a lot less gas, and I simply love them.

My nephews, I call them all like they were, do also enjoy a good pint and we have some happy times together. After some chats and a few beers, well maybe more than just a few, off we go to Craven Cottage where the newcomers Nicola and Aaron have never been but they're already following Fulham. Good boys.

We also have a special guest today, and it's time for my namesake. Little Simone, the son of my good friends Tiziana and Pier, who now live in London, is going to come with us. Some family friends are trying to infect him with the Chelsea virus but I'll do my best to keep him clean and follow the best club in west London.

Wigan are struggling in the table but anyone who thinks it's going to be easy today can't be more wrong.

Fulham start well and little winger Ayité puts us in front after a good pass from Aluko. The celebration goes on while Nicola and Aaron are probably still enjoying the ground and being so close to the actual pitch. The happiness is short-lived though as Wigan turn the game in their favour with Malone's own goal and Jacobs's strike with the last kick of the first half.

Excitement is still in our eyes but you'd prefer a win, especially for them in their first game here. The second half is dominated by the Whites and in the 71st minute Odoi with a screamer from long out equalises.

Fulham press high and dominate possession then, in the 93rd minute, Cairney plays Kebano in. His quick feet leave the defender begging and he slots in the winning goal. Of course it's madness in the Hammersmith End. I'm embracing my boys and we're jumping around and screaming in joy.

Of course the lucky gates ritual had been restored and the result was a logical outcome.

Beers flow in the Railway as we get back there to celebrate. Happy faces all over. We say goodbye to Jeff who has got a train to catch and we move to the local KFC. I'm a healthy person who usually follows a good diet but there are two things I indulge myself in a couple of times a year: Kentucky Fried Chicken, God bless the colonel, and M&M's!

It's all laughter while we jump on to the basket full of goodness. My nephew Nicola had a beer too many and is struggling a bit so he's not having food. I have to make sure that my sister doesn't read this book.

They go back to their place and I take the train towards Balham, as usual reading the match programme. Finally in bed, my light goes off and I fall asleep with a big smile on my face.

It's Sunday in London and as I catch up with the boys I'm updated on the guest house. The water in the shower was cold, and a cold shower in a cold bathroom is not what you wish for after a day out like ours. Anyway, off we go, enjoying good pub food and some lovely ales. On Monday they want to go to Millwall. I'm curious too and so we reach Bermondsey. After actually walking a bit too much from the train station we get to The Den, home of the Lions. There are not many people around so we take a look and see one of the big gates is open, and we're in. A worker is watering the pitch and we ask if we can have a look around. Approved. We take some pictures, visit the little shop and think it'd be good to come down here for a match once.

Under the famous, or infamous, tunnel, I take a picture of the boys so they can tell their football friends back home they've been there too.

We get back to central London for food and after a decent pint off we go to Arsenal. The boys tour the Emirates and we then move down to Balham to meet up with Mr Cook who takes us to my favourite curry place in London, the Indian Room. There's still the same waiter since the old days, he recognises me, we sit down and enjoy a great meal. Saag gosht and peshwari naan for me please. The lamb is so tender here I could eat it forever. It's the perfect way to end a good Monday so bring on Tuesday – match day.

We have a late lunch, chill down a bit and by 5pm we're in the Railway waiting for Mark to join us. The pub is slowly becoming full of our colours, a thing I so badly miss back there in Mallorca. I love the sun and the beach but a day at the pub is unbeatable.

A few beers later we're ready to take on the streets and once more reach my beloved Craven Cottage. By night it's even more magic; it's simply amazing in the floodlights with the River Thames next to it. The boys love it too and I'm so proud they're having a good time. Plus it's Valentine's Day so please, Fulham, get me a nice gift.

This time we face Forest where our former winger Kasami is now playing. And of course he scores. We get in a little late and hear the noise and the screams from the outside; it's not loud so we must be behind. We are, after just two minutes. If there's something that really gets on my nerves it's missing the kick-off, even on TV.

But we play well, the passing is fluid, we look dangerous and within half an hour we've turned the game around. A good combination down the left means Cairney is able to place his shot from inside the penalty area then Piazon becomes a skier and slaloms past a few defenders before coolly converting with his left. Almost with the first kick after the interval though, Forest equalise. A good cross from the left finds giant youngster

Ben Brereton unmarked. His header is very good and Button is beaten as the few away supporters applaud again. The game is a little nervy and we're no longer confident but we've Saint Kebano in our ranks. After coming off the bench just a few minutes earlier he scores the 3-2 winner for the second game running. The goal will be later considered an own goal and it's a pity for our little number seven who would have deserved the victory honour again.

In the end what counts is the three points and the fact we've won the two home games we had the chance to play in succession. This calls for a beer, doesn't it?

It's been a great long weekend of football, beer and friends. Nicola and Aaron loved London and Fulham, which is great for me – I had few doubts to be honest. Little Simone loved his time at Craven Cottage and hopefully he'll love Fulham from now on.

So, see you soon to them and to London. I fly back to Palma super happy: six points in the bag for Fulham, some memorabilia in my luggage, KFC, great ales and a lovely curry. All I needed from London, I got. I couldn't wish for more.

Fulham then make three in three with a 2-0 win at Bristol City with the in-form Piazon and Cairney scoring. We're flying. Jokanović's ideas seem all to be absorbed by his players. The following week brings another good away result, this time 2-2 at Cardiff. Kebano gets the equalising goal.

The first game of March provides another win, 3-1 at the Cottage over Preston with Aluko, Martin and Kebano scoring. We're now seventh and a play-off spot is within reach. Ream's own goal dents our run early on during the visit of Leeds but Cairney levels in the very last minute, joyful. Morale is sky-high and you can tell it when we demolish Newcastle, the top of the class. At St James' Park it's a rampant 3-1 for the boys with Sessegnon bagging his first senior brace after another Cairney goal, in front of 52,000 spectators.

Another entertaining home draw brings one more point after a 2-2 with Blackburn, Ivorian loanee Cyriac with the only goal of his short Fulham career. Our eight-game unbeaten run then comes to an end at home at the hands of Wolves who deservedly beat us 3-1. We promptly bounce back to win at Rotherham, Aluko's effort enough for the three points.

My Saturday schedule is clear: sleep until late, and besides finishing work at around 1am or 2am, I'm training for the New York City Marathon which will take place in November. It's part of the Master's in Coaching I'm studying. I have a good breakfast or even some pasta then head to the Lennox for the Fulham game.

An in-form Derby County, under new management, give us a reality check when thanks to David Nugent's hat-trick they beat us 4-2.

But instead of crashing, Fulham regain shape and go into a massive four wins in a row. The first three are all 3-1, against Ipswich and Aston Villa at the Cottage and Norwich at Carrow Road. That was not an easy task in Norfolk, especially with a man down. Then, on 22 April, we run riot in Huddersfield, with a 4-1 win. Full-back Malone scores his second in four, Cairney nets his second successful penalty in three, and Johansen adds a brace. It's a great win over a direct rival for a play-off place.

We're the Championship's top scorers, and definitely best entertainers too I'd add. We're sixth in the table and Leeds are three points below us.

Cairney scores again but it's just a 1-1 draw at home to Brentford before the Whites, even if playing in red, are back to winning ways in the first game of May when Kebano's double seals the 2-1 away win at Sheffield Wednesday. We finish sixth and the play-offs are confirmed.

I'm super happy. Slav's class worked out well in the end, we're a joy to watch and definitely a team no one would like to face. But a poor refereeing performance against Reading sinks our promotion hopes. The 1-1 draw by the Thames in the first leg is followed by a 1-0 defeat at the Madejski Stadium three days later thanks to Kermorgant's penalty.

I'm sick. Former Manchester United and Lazio defensive wall Jaap Stam's men carry on while we will play one more season in the Championship. Awful!

Fulham dominated the first half of the home clash but missed too many opportunities. In the second half Reading took the lead after two clear fouls on Fulham players right in front of the shambolic Stuart Attwell. Cairney equalised after a well orchestrated move down the left.

In the second leg, keepers starred until the moment Martin Atkinson pointed to the spot for a Reading penalty. Kalas got clearly pushed and the ball hit his hand while he had anticipated the attacker. But the ref decided he wanted a part in the plot so he blew the whistle. Bettinelli guessed correctly but was unlucky as the ball beat him. Reading then missed a glorious chance with a counter attack, as did Piazon moments later. Reading goalkeeper Al-Habsi then held firm with probably his performance of a lifetime and there were no further goals.

I remember being so pissed off when I rewatched the game at home after work that I wanted to throw the laptop from the window. Luckily I didn't and I'm now writing this with it.

We stay in the Championship and there's no promotion party, no Manchester United, no visits to Stamford Bridge or Spurs at home, and no 'You'll Never Walk Alone' live at Anfield. Another tough season with loads of games, very often every three days, with the visiting end quite empty most of the time.

Vicenza have been in the lower leagues long enough that I can't stand them much nowadays so to see Fulham in the second tier hurts me.

But I keep my faith in Slav. We have a nice style of play, we entertain, we score goals, and supporters have their pride and enthusiasm back. This year we didn't make it but I'm still confident that the only way is up.

It's July, it's hot and humid, work is frenetic but satisfying then it's once again Facebook, the social network invented to connect to people, who gives me bad news.

Mark, a friend from the UK, tells me Giampaolo has been found dead. I have to sit and read it again. In the meantime the phone rings and it's a friend from Italy. Paolo was his best man at the wedding, and I quickly realise it has really happened. We're both crying, thousands of kilometres away.

I hang up and crash on the sofa, and quickly all memories about our friendship come up. His contagious smile and nice wave. Everybody loved him. I reckon he's the most genuine person I've ever met.

Immediately my mind goes to Gill and little Leonardo because yes, Giampaolo did marry that girl he dated on my birthday years ago. And they had a son, a marvellous boy.

Giampaolo only met his father in the early 2000s. He always suffered about it and his main aim and wish in life was to have a family and become a father – a better one than his.

He did that and he was over the moon every time we talked, constantly mentioning Gill and Leo. He eventually had his dream come true and then fate hit them so unfairly.

I call home and tell my mum what happened and she's touched. She goes on recalling when Giampaolo was coming home for dinner and embracing her as if she was like an auntie or similar.

When I get to work I again fall into tears, telling Luigi I have to leave in two days for the funeral. Once landed in Gatwick I still feel so weird. It's like being in a bubble. I look at other travellers, so many different faces, different colours and no, I'm not going to see Paolo's any more.

I meet up with Mr Cook and Terry arrives to pick us up. The day goes on recalling all our time with Paolo. Our trips to Iceland where the airport police took a lot of the beer we bought at the duty free. Thank God my luggage was the one we stuffed with spirits. But they only stopped Paolo.

Then Kiev, or the amazing week we spent in Tuscany where we rented a van and travelled the whole region enjoying amazing food and wine with Paolo always waking everybody up with Lady Gaga's 'Poker Face'!

Terry used to call Paolo 'Buffon' as he was the keeper of the Copthorne Rovers, the amateur team Terry managed.

Personally, I still go back in time thinking about our car trip from Vicenza to London. It was the sort of thing I wish everybody could experience once in a lifetime. I recall our night shifts at the military base playing *FIFA* and the incredible amount of coffee Paolo could down!

Even if I try to control myself I cannot hide the tears when I look at Leonardo playing and I hug him as if he had my own blood.

Susan, Rachel's mum, recalls how much of her delicious rogan josh me and Paolo once ate at her house while Pino remembers the World Cup Final at his restaurants and how Paolo loved his country. Being away it doesn't mean you have to forget where you came from and to win such an important football competition was immense for us expats.

Giampaolo incredibly died of pneumonia in his sleep on 12 July 2017. July, the month we celebrated Italy reaching the top of world football from the top of Pino's restaurant. It's too easy to say we touched the sky with our hands but that night it really happened.

Flying back to Mallorca, I think about how I've lost two of my best mates in such a short period of time. Two great buddies I've shared and enjoyed a very important chapter of my life with. A good night out, taking life with a smile and loving football were all things we had in common.

Paolo had asked me to be Leonardo's godfather, something I would have loved to be but unfortunately because of work, I could not. I still regret that a lot.

Early Scare and the Bid for Joy

Soundtrack: 'Stairway to Heaven'
– Led Zeppelin

IF IT'S summer, you work in a restaurant and you live in Mallorca, running with the perfect weather conditions is almost impossible. Between 5am and 7am temperatures are bearable, but I finish working by 1am. After seven in the morning the heat is crazy and humidity peaks to silly levels. So what I do is wake up by 8am and go. My training schedule is getting tough now with around 50km to do per week. I've never been a distance runner, I'm more a sprinter, and I'm used to keeping myself fit with 5km twice a week together with regular gym visits.

But I've a target and I have to run the NYC Marathon within four hours and 30 minutes. Sometimes, if I feel it, I even go just after work. It's funny because I'm there running at 2am bumping into drunks or stoned people going around the city's clubs.

Fulham's new kit is clean. I like its simplicity. The away shirt is black and the third is still the red one. A good combination.

Our captain, Scott Parker, retires, so it's farewell to a great servant, and the transfer window is far from exciting. French forward Yohan Mollo comes in on a free, while we add Spanish defender Marcelo Djaló, midfielder Ibrahima Cissé and two forwards, Aboubakar Kamara and Rui Fonte. Fonte is the brother of Southampton defender José and has a past in the Arsenal youth system. The good business comes this time from the loans as Piazon and Kalas are back again and we also bag central midfielder Oliver Norwood from Brighton. Liverpool starlet Sheyi Ojo is also signed temporarily. The squad is trimmed with non-regulars leaving the club. It's a pity to see Lasse Christensen leaving permanently while Sone Aluko is lured to Reading and Scott Malone is rewarded for his brilliant past season with the call from promoted Huddersfield Town. We also loan in young defender Rafa Soares from Porto.

Pre-season friendlies are forgettable, although any 4-2 win over QPR is always something to enjoy. We are again among the favourites for promotion even if I feel we lack a proper goalscorer, a forward who'll get those 15 goals or so to propel the entire team. Let's see. I'll get behind the lads as usual.

Three draws and one defeat to start the season is a return that surprises many. In the two home games against Norwich and Sheffield Wednesday we only get one point with a 1-1 draw on the opening day against the Canaries. The Owls steal the points with Steven Fletcher's 64th-minute goal. Away, we draw with ten men at Reading, who lost to Huddersfield in the play-off final, thanks to Piazon's goal, then it's 0-0 at Leeds.

The last game of August marks our first win, a 2-0 raid at Ipswich with Fonte scoring his first goal. Unfortunately we still have to wait for the first home win of the campaign when we're held 1-1 at the Cottage by Cardiff with Sessegnon opening his account for the season. But the desired win comes only four days later anyway, at the expense of newly relegated Hull City. Ayité and Johansen score to make it seven points in three after a difficult start and maybe get us thinking we're back on track. The following 2-1 defeat at Burton is a heavy punch in the stomach and a very bad performance at the Pirelli Stadium rises fierce criticism among pundits and fans.

The following week the boys are not able to get their heads up again and they have to cope with a 1-1 home draw with Middlesbrough.

It's almost the end of September and we only have 11 points. It's a corner we have to turn if we really are in for another try at promotion, as getting so behind early on can prove very dangerous later on.

The message seems to be received by the Whites as they gather seven points in the next three games. They win 3-1 at Nottingham Forest and then 2-1 at QPR, but we still struggle at home and only draw 2-2 against Preston with Odoi rescuing a point in the 96th minute.

Jokanović's men can't find the form they showed in the last campaign and we're struggling for goals. The following five games see us only drawing two and losing three, a tally which is definitely not acceptable, and there are even rumours of the Khan family considering sacking Slav. Visits to Villa Park and Molineux are also unproductive, losing 2-1 at Villa with former Chelsea captain John Terry getting one for the hosts and 2-0 at Wolves who just need 26 minutes to put the game to bed. Bristol City come away from Stevenage Road with a 2-0 win. We draw the other two home games, both 1-1, with Bolton and Derby.

It's not good enough. We're nowhere near our sparkling football and up front the likes of Fonte and Kamara seem clearly out of their depth.

I'm in New York for the marathon and I'm quite happy I can't watch both defeats. On Sunday, 5 November, we get up really early. It's a poor day in the Big Apple but at least it's not raining. Once we reach the starting point it's simply overwhelming with all these people from all over the world, here for probably the most important running competition on the planet.

By the time I'm almost halfway through, the big screens on the street show Kenyan Geoffrey Kamworor winning it in just two hours, ten minutes and 53 seconds.

Anyway, I did my best too and also thanks to Andrea Cosentino, my Masters mate and marathon buddy, I touch the end line in four hours 22 minutes and 24 seconds. I've spent the last 100m walking, soaking up the public support and cheering, with colleagues calling my name. It's so powerful and immense. It's true what they told us beforehand that when you complete a marathon you'll feel like everything is possible. You'll feel like a superhero!

When I fly back to Palma, I hang up my medal on the bedroom wall to remind me every morning what I can achieve.

I do hope Fulham can complete their marathon, because it's mid-November and we're 17th. Relegation is looming. I struggle to believe it. My mate at work is teasing me and I really hate it when others mock my Fulham. But the boys need to wake up and Slav has to find the way to go back to the old days when watching them playing was a joy. I can't see us in the Championship, so imagine if we were to go down to League One.

Then a thrilling 5-4 win at Sheffield United is the turning point of the season:

6: Clarke, 1-0
28: Ojo, 1-1
30: Sessegnon, 1-2
39: Clarke, 2-2
43: Sessegnon, 2-3
69: Ojo, 2-4
78: Sessegnon, 2-5

86: Carruthers, 3-5

90+1: Clarke, 4-5

It's an epic game of pure football with no defensive desire and we manage to hold on to go back to London with the three points.

It's a nice half of the month because I'm also back home where I'm officially launching my first book, a novel based on my mum's tales. The live presentation is attended by over 70 people and I'm honestly touched. I'm not Ken Follett or Irvine Welsh but I'm super glad to see all these people here for it.

Fully rewarded by the success of the book night, I'm back to London when Oliver Norwood, who's proving to be our best signing so far, coolly takes the penalty which wins us the home derby with Millwall, closing a good month of November.

Odoi's red card is key in our 3-1 debacle at Brentford in the first game of December, but we then bounce back with Ojo's only goal proving enough in the 1-0 home win over Birmingham. We lose 1-0 at struggling Sunderland to a goal by our former academy player and London-born striker Josh Maja. We again get back on our feet with a 2-1 win over Barnsley, Ojo and Ayité scoring, and beat Cardiff 4-2 in Wales. Ream, Ayité, Sessegnon and Johansen are our goal heroes.

Point number ten of the last month of the year comes from the entertaining 2-2 draw away to Hull, Kamara proving the unlikely star with a brace from 2-0 down.

And to mark the turn of the year, January brings four league games – and four league wins.

Fulham being at their best means ball possession, defences being torn apart and goals galore.

There's a narrow 1-0 win at Middlesbrough thanks to a calmly converted 95th-minute penalty by the ever important

Norwood, but Fulham then thrash, in order, Ipswich, Burton and Barnsley.

The Tractor Boys are well beaten 4-1 on a cold night at Craven Cottage. Sessegnon, now playing as a wing-back, and Kamara, both score a brace. Home fans are again delighted with the 6-0 destruction of Burton when even Fonte manages two goals, Sessegnon repeats his feat, and Kamara and Piazon bag one apiece. The away rout at Oakwell sees the third brace by Ryan Sessegnon in four games while there's deserved recognition for one of our unsung heroes, McDonald, with the effective winner in the 92nd minute.

Twelve points out of 12, full houses, things are going great and a firecracker comes in on the last day of the transfer window when striker Aleksandar Mitrović, a Serbian international, joins on loan from Premier League new boys Newcastle. This is a statement of intent and Jokanović should now have his real number nine. Young left-back Matt Targett is also a potentially good signing while misfit Mollo is released after a bunch of forgettable games.

The future looks pretty, my friends. Stay tuned.

The Unbeaten Run

Soundtrack: 'Invincible' – Tool

I SPENT the festive period at home with my family, which always recharges me physically and spiritually. I've also managed to watch some of the games with my nephews while planning for our next visit to London.

I've also decided to leave Bunker's as working with friends is like a coin, it has two sides. Once back in Mallorca I'll apply for a few job opportunities and see. Thankfully there's plenty of work on the island and my CV is quite good.

Let's focus back on Fulham anyway because this could be the season we eventually regain our Premier League status. Waiting for some replies to my job applications, I find some incredibly cheap flights to London while googling in my spare time. I check the fixtures and book immediately – I'm going to be there for the home game versus Forest.

After the goal fest of January, the Whites start February with the right foot and beat Forest with a neat 2-0 after Piazon and Johansen score. Another three points on my visit to the Cottage! Jeff and Mark are teasing me once more about the lucky gates routine but also happy it's bringing good luck to Fulham.

In Bolton we can't keep our 1-0 lead with Targett's first goal in our colours, drawing 1-1, but we're straight back to winning days in the following home game. Now Craven Cottage is again a place where opponents are quite afraid to visit and we beat Villa 2-0, Sessegnon and Ayité again starring.

It's 1-1 once more on the road as Mitrović opens his Fulham account at Bristol City. But the game I'm looking forward to is not this one, it's the home visit of Wolverhampton Wanderers. Me and the boys are going to be there.

Ryanair flights this time of the year are very cheap and Mallorca is so well connected that I fly home so I can then jump on the plane to London together with the boys. This time, alongside my nephew Nicola and his best mate – also Nicola – there will be Luca, Samuele and another Luca. The Fulham-supporting group is growing fast.

We're 20 minutes after leaving home when I realise I've left my passport at my mum's. I make a U-turn while the boys take the piss, but thankfully we've got plenty of time and we reach the airport with no rush.

When we land in Stansted it's a cold winter afternoon. We're all staying close together in Clapham and our first stop is the Windmill pub because it's nearby. It's around 4pm but the kitchen is still open, so we're lucky. The waitress looks at us quite suspiciously, or, well, let's say a little annoyedly. I read something like, 'Look at these six Italians coming in late, they're going to keep me here long for nothing.' Oh, if that was really what she thought, she couldn't have been more wrong.

We're cold, hungry, but most of all, thirsty and so looking forward to a good pint of ale. We down our first pint in a world-record time and when she comes back to our table to take the food order you can clearly tell she's surprised and a smile is back on her face. She writes down our choices and we make clear we need her around often because we're going to drink. A lot. Please.

One hour later and we're in heaven; a satisfied stomach is pampered with pints of ales at such a pace that it looks like we fear there's not going to be beer in the world any more.

The cold outside is well forgotten as venison burgers, fish and chips and beef pies restore the good mood. The ale helps too.

Everybody's happy; us because we are properly fed and can also enjoy some great ales after a while, and the waitress because we keep her entertained and leave a nice tip. The owners because the bill is fat.

We spend the Friday night around Clapham Common and Clapham South station. It's good to go out here and I know a few places from my time in Balham. We sleep late into Saturday morning and we reach the Rocket pub by Putney Bridge when it's not even midday.

Unfortunately the iconic Railway closed its doors forever last September after 24 years of service. It goes without saying that I was sad about that. I have so many good memories from there, and I was even more unhappy when I saw they opened up another soulless fancy club in there.

The Rocket is still new. The area was revamped not long ago, some apartments with great views surround it, and it's a good pub. Good ales are served and the capacity is quite big. As we get in my mate Jeff is there waiting for us; it's always a joy to see him.

We get our first round of pints and get on chatting while the pub fills up. It's a big game as Wolves are top of the table with a squad that could do well in the Premier League without a doubt.

Time goes by, a certain happiness fuelled by good booze helps in the cold, the short walk is animated by chants of 'Come on you Whites!' resounding here and there through Bishops Park. If the players are fired up as we are, Wolves have no chance.

The ritual of the gates has been respected once again, I purchase the match programme at the usual stand, the one by the corner of Greswell Street, and Craven Cottage is as beautiful as ever. Season ticket holders greet their neighbours as we go to our seats in the Hammersmith End. The match hasn't started yet and we notice some empty seats closer to the front. We're within a couple of metres of the pitch; this is something the boys absolutely love. Entrance music plays loud and the two teams come out the tunnel. Luca and Samuele are just taking in the atmosphere and keep looking left and right, commenting on how amazing the old ground is, how much they like this and that of the British football compared to how it is back home in Italy.

Our line-up is our regular one with the starting XI in a 4-3-3 formation made of Bettinelli in goal, Fredericks, Kalas, Ream and Targett the back four, Cairney, McDonald and Johansen in the middle, with Ayité and Ryan Sessegnon flanking Mitrović. Norwood and Odoi are among the substitutes.

Diogo Jota is on the bench for Wolves while Rúben Neves, one of their many new signings, is suspended. To give you an idea of how strong this Wolves side is, Neves has played Champions League football with Porto and many big names were after him. They're also managed by Nuno Espírito Santo, who has previously been in charge of Valencia and Porto. He has taken Wolves to the top of the Championship and they have a nine-point cushion on second-placed Cardiff.

The first half is entertaining and the two teams show why they're promotion candidates, then in the 38th minute Johansen plays a good ball through for Mitrović, who quickly turns and shoots. John Ruddy can only parry the shot and Sessegnon is the quickest on the loose ball to tap in. It's madness in the Hammersmith End as we grab each other and start screaming.

Ah, the joy of a goal, if only there was a word to properly explain it. It remains 1-0 to Fulham at the interval.

A visit to the stadium toilet is needed after all the pints downed at the Rocket and once back we chat over the first period. The second half gets under way and the tension is mounting. I promise my nephew and his friends that if we win and get promoted, we'll all get a Fulham tattoo and I'll pay for it.

In the 71st minute Johansen passes to Mitro, who is just outside the box. He turns and shrugs off Coady then plays a dummy and shoots a low drive which ends up in the bottom corner. May the party time begin! Almost everybody is going crazy as celebrations kick off while during ours I get accidentally elbowed in the mouth by Luca, who breaks my upper lip. Who cares, we're dominating the league leaders. Johansen, probably the man of the match for me, goes close to a third and well-deserved goal but 2-0 it remains.

Uncountable pints flood the Rocket for the post-match celebrations and I wonder how Jeff will manage to get on the right train. The boys are super happy as am I. It's the eighth victory in a row at the Cottage for Fulham. We're unbeaten in 12 and now just five points away from the automatic promotion places.

The momentum sees us win another three games in a row. Derby are conquered 2-1 with Mitro and Sessegnon again banging the goals and the big Serbian gets a brace in the 3-0 home disposal of Sheffield United, with Cairney back on the score sheet. Our signature 2-1 win is back soon afterwards thanks to Mitro's brace at Preston, and we're fourth in the league.

Our WhatsApp chat with the nephews is smoking hot, enthusiasm is sky high and every result is commented on with joy. I couldn't be happier.

The winning streak is momentarily interrupted by the home draw with QPR, which really annoys me as the Whites throw away a two-goal half-time lead. Cairney and Piazon score but in the second half we briefly switch off and QPR punish us. Slav is annoyed and I reckon he made himself clear at Motspur Park because the boys promptly go out with another four wins in a row, all without conceding a goal!

Jokanović's football vision is definitely paying off. He stuck to his ideas and now we're almost unbeatable. The ball possession stats are incredible, Kalas and Ream look like a wall, Cairney is directing the game with class, Sessegnon is blossoming and Mitro is simply flawless. We beat Norwich 2-0 at Carrow Road and Leeds by the same score at the Cottage, while two 1-0 victories see off Wednesday in Sheffield and Reading in London. I'm pleased, particularly for the fourth win. The bitter taste of last season's play-off semi-final hasn't entirely gone so beating them gives me pleasure.

In these four fixtures, Mitrović has got two more goals, as has Johansen. The Norwegian captain and McDonald are the perfect pairing to Cairney's style of play.

Once again, our streak is broken by a west London rival as Brentford draw at Craven Cottage. This time is even worse because Maupay's goal comes in the 94th minute when almost everybody was ready to celebrate a fifth win in a row. Damn. It's a bad result because we could have got back to second in the table, especially as Cardiff have also a game in hand over us.

Anyway, I can't be unhappy can I? We haven't lost a game in ages and are playing so brilliantly that if we had done this from the beginning of the season we would have probably beaten our record points tally of 101. I'm optimistic, however. Getting automatic promotion is tough because Wolves are now safely up and Cardiff are scraping wins here and there. Neil Warnock's style of play can't be compared with ours but he's an old fox who knows the league well so it will be very hard to get second spot.

Personally, I've started working for a luxury catering company and it's fun. I'm meeting some new people and this will allow me to travel a lot around the island, seeing amazing villas and posh places. I've also worked at Newcastle owner Mike Ashley's wife's birthday party. You can definitely tell they splashed the cash as Mark Ronson was the DJ and David Walliams gave the birthday speech. My mind went back to my London days, great memories. I used to love *Little Britain*.

Living in Palma is cool. My flat is in a residential area, very quiet and safe but within walking distance to all amenities. Now I will also have more time for me, not that I didn't before but there will be more nights free.

That also means more chances to watch Fulham's games, like the 3-0 thrashing of Millwall at The Den on 20 April with Sess and Mitro scoring again. Or the 2-1 win over derelict Sunderland the following Saturday. The already relegated Black Cats took the lead but Piazon's sitter and Mitro's header secure another win for us. We're now second with one game to play while Cardiff have two. And we have a two-point advantage.

The Bluebirds still have to face Hull and Reading while Fulham will travel to Birmingham for their last game.

Unfortunately a spirited display by Birmingham on the final day means a 3-1 defeat for the Whites and the end of any automatic promotion hopes. Cardiff finish second, two points above us.

We Are Premier League

Soundtrack: 'Party Rock Anthem' – LMFAO

THE UNBELIEVABLE 23-match unbeaten run came to an end in the worst possible way. But hey, keep those heads up, we finish third and that means home advantage in the play-off semi-final against sixth-placed Derby County.

The away match is planned for 11 May so I check my working schedule and fuck, I've got a service. I'm new in the company so I try sniffing around to see if there's any chance for a swap but no. Damn. Probably the disappointment in not getting promoted is still nagging the boys and the performance shows it in the first leg. It's 1-0 Derby, the experienced Cameron Jerome with the decisive goal. I can't think about another semi-final exit.

Please no. For the second leg the Cottage is packed and almost all seats are gone. It's Monday night and I'm in the Lennox, my lucky Mallorcan pub, in the company of my mate and namesake Simone. No, not the little kid from London, but a mate I got to know in Palma. He's a Lazio fan, we've developed a good friendship this year and he's here to support. I'm wearing this year's black kit with Cairney 10 printed on, bought during my last visit to the club shop. There's a bloke in a Derby kit entering the place with who I suppose is his girlfriend. I politely nod, he doesn't. I sneer and laugh. And I laugh louder and louder at the final whistle; it's 2-0 Fulham. It's Wembley!

The guy leaves irritated, I cheer with my mate. Sessegnon, one of my season MVPs, has opened the score and Odoi's header has sealed our place in the play-off final.

Amazing! I check flights and dates but again, it's almost impossible for me to be there. It's high season at work and they've just promoted me to maître d' so I can't travel. It's Fulham's third-most important final after the 1975 FA Cup Final, the year I was born, and the 2010 Europa League one. Fulham have lost both.

The big game will take place on 26 May at Wembley. Aston Villa are a historic club in world football, not only in England. In 1982 they won the European Cup, now called Champions League, and they have seven English championships, and seven FA Cups, five League Cups and one European Super Cup. A big, big club.

In the past few years they've been up and down but this year they have some good players. John Terry is past his best but his leadership and experience can prove vital in the Championship. In Jack Grealish they surely have a pure talent who'll soon wear the England team's shirt, while midfielders Mile Jedinak, Robert Snodgrass and Conor Hourihane are a luxury in this league. It's going to be a tough call for my beloved Fulham. But they can do it.

My mates Jeff and Mark are going and I'm so happy for them. I genuinely envy them, in a nice way. I've asked Jeff to get me the match programme. I won't even be able to watch the game as I'll be working. I've good feelings but I'm going to keep that for me.

When we stayed up thanks to Roy Hodgson's men's great escape I was a guest at a wedding. This time I'll be again at a wedding, working, making sure the couple have the best day of their lives, while hoping all my Fulham friends at the game will have theirs.

So, it's easy to describe what an infinite huge relief and feeling of happiness it was for me when I checked my phone and found the messages saying we'd won and Fulham were promoted back to the Premier League!

Once the event ended I immediately went on Facebook to watch videos taken from the ground. There were 85,000 people at Wembley, among them the White Wall, our huge presence in the stands, and no name would have been better. It was really impressive in videos and pictures so I can only imagine how amazing it was live. I can't wait to hear it from Jeff. I've watched Cairney's goal over and over again! What a pass from Sess, what a cool finish from Tom. Our captain with the promotion goal, how's that for a tale?

We're back where we belong. The Premier League is our place and I do hope the Khan family will give Jokanović the squad he deserves. We've been by far the most entertaining team in the league and only a bad start stopped us getting automatic promotion. But we've won the play-off final and a windfall of money will land into the club's bank accounts. We all know how TV rights are now the major income and there's no comparison to the real money you get once in the Premier League, the best and most followed league in the world.

Scenes of the boys celebrating on the pitch, Betts filled with joy running around holding flares, the memory of 'Bruce Odoi Lee' taking down Grealish, the commentator calling it 'a fabulous day for Fulham', JT's sad face. Oh dear, oh dear. An unforgettable day for sure.

And me, proudly walking around Palma's streets in my Fulham kit. We are Premier League people, we're back.

I proudly state my Fulham support to all surprised customers when I get to talk about football. A lot of British come to Mallorca for weddings so every time the matter comes up I always say Fulham with a smile on my face. Some are telling me they're pleased to see us back there. Then one day there's a bunch of guests talking about the other club in Fulham Road. They think I'm Spanish and go on guessing if I'm Real or Barcelona, or Mallorca, living here. I wait for the right time and there goes my sucker punch, 'I'm a Fulham fan, and we're back.' I'd love for you to see their faces. The smirk is almost instantly gone while I leave laughing in tears.

Moneyball

Soundtrack: 'Money for Nothing'
– Dire Straits

OUR 2018 summer transfer campaign will stay in the record books, and unfortunately our memories, as probably the worst waste of money ever. Or, let me correct myself, the worst-run transfer campaign ever. Let's put it like that. Mind you, it only really becomes the case afterwards.

From 12 July the club starts spending a fortune on new players. A newly promoted team surpassing £100m spending. Wow.

I must admit I was pleased to see our management finally splashing the cash, as analysts say we have one of the richest owners in the Premier League. At the same time, I don't see the sense of many of our transfers.

The first big-name signing is Jean Michaël Seri, an Ivorian international, who has been on Barcelona's radar for a while with praise coming even from such a name as Xavi. He costs £18m plus add-ons from Nice together with club-mate Maxime Le Marchand, a left-back who can operate also in a central position. A few days later, experienced Spanish keeper Fabri comes in from Beşiktaş for a rumoured fee of around £4m.

Then former Chelsea attacker and World Cup winner André Schürrle is signed on loan from Borussia Dortmund.

And the 30th is the day every Fulham fan is waiting for as promotion star Aleksandar Mitrović is back at the club on a permanent basis after a £22m cheque has gone to Newcastle United. Social media is invaded by jubilant posts.

During the first ten days of August there are times where I think we could sign anybody. Centre-backs Alfie Mawson, who was doing well at Swansea before injuring his knee, and Calum Chambers join for £15m plus add-ons and on loan from Arsenal respectively. Exciting left-back Joe Bryan is in from Bristol City for £6m and Cameroon hot prospect André-Frank Zambo Anguissa makes the move from French giants Marseille for a fee believed to be in the region of £30m. Incredible.

Young right-back Timothy Fosu-Mensah, a Dutch international, is loaned from Manchester United while Spanish keeper Sergio Rico also comes in on loan from Sevilla where he twice won the Europa League.

Luciano Vietto, an Argentine forward, also joins on loan from Atlético Madrid on the same day having previously played for Valencia and Sevilla.

Manchester United, Sevilla, Atlético Madrid, Arsenal, Marseille, Borussia Dortmund, Chelsea. Hey, wait a minute, these are all football superpowers who usually buy from us, whenever they want. And now we're knocking at their doors asking, 'How much is that guy?' and writing big cheques. What's going on? Are the Khan family doing what Mo Al-Fayed once promised? Are we going to be the Manchester United of the south?

As the disbelief goes though, I sit down and think properly. We have Bettinelli, a young lad, one of our own who did so well in the Championship. Okay, getting a more experienced keeper from whom he can learn makes sense, so why two? Sergio Rico is well known, has got European pedigree and I'm still unsure why he's here. He's definitely on a hefty wage so why also sign Fabri?

Odoi has surpassed Kalas in Slav's pecking order but the former Chelsea man and Ream formed a great pair at the centre of our defence, although we all know that's where we will need reinforcement of the highest calibre. The Premier League is ruthless and at the heart of your defence you need to be strong. And we sign Mawson who hasn't played for ages and is still recovering from the injury. Plus, we don't get Kalas permanently. And we sign Chambers, who's mainly a right-back and didn't look so secure at Arsenal.

Midfield is where people always say you win games. And we spend a fortune on two promising players, yes, I'll give you that, who come from another league. They'll need to instantly adjust to the pace and physicality of the Premier League.

I don't know. I'm as usual optimistic and I keep telling my nephews that we should be fine and good value for mid-table.

Marseille fans are sending thankful messages towards our management for taking Anguissa away. For £30m, mind you. It seems Mr Khan has a team of analysts giving him lists of data-effective players to be signed. Have you ever watched *Moneyball* with Brad Pitt? It's a true story and a great motivational movie where a baseball manager builds his team using the same tools and logic. It goes pretty well for him. But that's baseball. A totally different sport.

I don't know how much say Jokanović had in all these signings. It's a good thing we managed to hold on to our hot prospect and young jewel Ryan Sessegnon who incredibly was our top scorer last season.

There are also some departures. I almost forgot it with all these millions going out. Ryan Fredericks joins West Ham on a free and this puzzles me a bit. David Button leaves for Brighton with not many of us regretting that, while Cauley Woodrow, who for me never really had a chance, moves to Barnsley. Young Slovakian keeper Marek Rodak is once again loaned out, as is Marcelo Djaló, who we've barely seen. The misfiring Rui Fonte joins Lille temporarily.

Working for the catering company is really satisfying, and sometimes very hard because events are long and we finish at five or six in the morning and the afternoon after we have another service. But it's good. I have a couple of new friends from Argentina, Mariano and Marcelo, and we really get on well from the beginning. Working for this company got me back to my London days as it's a melting pot of nationalities: Italy, Argentina, Canada, Spain, Paraguay, Senegal, Ghana. And there are plenty of hot colleagues which is always a plus.

Summer is blazing and humid but I love the sun and I get to travel the island and see nice properties and meet cool people. And the great news is that my nephew Nicola is coming to Mallorca on holiday with his mate Nicola. I'm very happy because the first week of August I'll be free as there are not many events due to the heat.

I like spending time with them because having been away for such a long time, I've missed their growing up. Now he's 21 we can do things together and he sees me as an older brother rather than an uncle. Some friends are surprised when he tells them he's going to London with his uncle or in this case, that he's going on holiday to see me. Then he shows them my pictures – thankfully I look younger than my age – and he tells them about Fulham or the exciting stuff I do and his friends are jealous. Ahahahahaha.

We have fun together. His birthday is on 5 August so I take them to a music festival, then we go out and about, I show them the island and I'm a bit sad when they leave.

The day after, Fulham kick off their return to the Premier League with a home game versus Crystal Palace. Tributes are paid to Roy Hodgson, who is now at Palace, and they are well deserved for what he did for us. Unfortunately he also leaves with all the points after a 2-0 win.

We are then beaten in a second straight London derby, 3-1 at White Hart Lane, Mitrović having levelled the game at one point.

Burnley at home is one I feel we can win and I'm off and free to watch it. Seri smashes in a screamer for the advantage, Hendrick quickly levels before Mitro's brace gives us the two-goal cushion. There are happy faces all around the Cottage even if Tarkowski gets one more for the visitors. The second half is quieter and Schürrle opens his Fulham account with the strike that seals the first three points of our new season.

You can tell how much people deserved a day like this after so many games in the Championship. I'm pleased and very happy for those who were there. They can now celebrate it with a beer and God only knows what I'd give to be among them.

I send a voice message to my nephews saying that with Ream back we'll be fine and fighting for a top-ten place. They still bring that up nowadays when they want to take the mickey out of me!

On 1 September we visit Brighton and we drop two points in a Fulhamish way, after being 2-0 up with Schürrle and Mitro scoring for the second game running. The first half is a show of what the boys can do as Betts saves a penalty and then Seri lobs a great pass into the box for Schürrle's easy tap-in. It's a glorious sunny afternoon on the south coast and Mitro takes advantage of a mistake in defence to double our lead. But then Le Marchand gives the ball away unexplainably and old poacher Murray punishes us.

And he does it again when Mitro is adjudged to have handballed inside our box. Murray blasts it in and it's points shared at the Amex. This is what I meant when saying that the Premier League is ruthless.

The following trip to the City of Manchester Stadium teaches the boys another serious lesson. It's 3-0 to the hosts and the pace and trickery of Leroy Sané, David Silva and Raheem Sterling prove a step too far.

The Whites miss a good chance to move up the table when they only draw 1-1 with Watford, Mitrović levelling Gray's early goal. But it's the six defeats in a row that eventually cost Slaviša Jokanović his job.

Here you can start a debate over whether it would be correct to give the manager a chance to impose his gameplay and ideas and adjust to the Premier League, or if it's better to act promptly so you could still have an opportunity to stay up. In my opinion Slav deserved more faith in him and should have had more of a voice in transfers, which we all know didn't happen.

His style might be too open for the Premier League but hey, he guided us to it with class, banging in goals and victories. It's quite clear our defence is unfortunately not good enough for this level. There was no time to gel with all the new faces.

Slav should have been given more time for me, especially when they replace him with Claudio Ranieri.

He's my countryman, I respect him; he did well when in charge of Juventus and some other Italian teams. He was the boss of Leicester City's Premier League win in 2016. But I simply don't see him as the right man for the job. I'm sorry and I'd be more than happy to be proven wrong. But I smell disaster.

The Tinkerman is appointed after a sequence of a 3-0 defeat at Everton, losing 5-1 at home to Arsenal, 4-2 at Cardiff, 3-0 to Bournemouth at the Cottage, 1-0 at Huddersfield, and 2-0 at Liverpool.

Above everything, the defensive woes are clear to see. Odoi, Le Marchand, Fosu-Mensah, Ream and Mawson are simply not Premier League material. Sorry, boys.

Fulham are bottom of the league. I'd like to cry, because you feel powerless, and you see that something is clearly wrong but you can't do anything more than getting behind the boys. Keep the faith. Still believe. Of course I'll do. But, hey, it's cruel.

Ranieri's first game in charge is at home to Southampton which is not impossible. Stuart Armstrong, another one who likes to score against us, puts the Saints in front early on. Mitro and Schürrle, our lights in these dark days, overturn that, only for Armstrong to level in the 53rd minute.

Craven Cottage's total joy coincides with Mitro's brace ten minutes later. My flatmate comes in from her bedroom with a sleepy face. I feel guilty but she smiles, 'You watching football?' We both laugh, I say sorry and that I can't promise to be quiet. I shut the door and she goes back to her nap. She's off today so no big deal.

It's a win. Well, Mr Ranieri, you've got a point, actually three, but you know what I mean. Let's celebrate and be happy at least for this weekend.

And I really hope I'll be happier the next one as once again my boys and I are going to be in London! I'm buzzing already.

London, Beers, Laughter and Tears

Soundtrack: 'The Boys Are Back in Town'
– Thin Lizzy

THIS TIME both my nephews, Manuel and Nicola, are going to be there, together with the other inseparables, Nicola and Luca Zoppi. Using my account, Jeff's, Mark's, Ben's and the generous help of Fulham fan James LS, who helped me out after my Facebook post on the Fulham Football Club page, we'll all be able to go to Stamford Bridge for the derby.

This time we'll all stay together in the same place. I've found a hostel which looks a good compromise between price, quality and location in Ealing. Me and Manuel will share one room, AND the two Nicolas and Luca will get the other. We'll all fly on Friday evening but I'll land earlier so I'LL go and sort everything out at the hostel then pick them up by Liverpool Street.

It's all hugs and pats on the back when we meet. I'm always so happy to see them and spending some time together in London is unique.

We find a place still open nearby and we celebrate the meeting with some beers. Unfortunately it's more like a club than a pub and they don't do draft beer but a bottled London Pride will work well. We reach Ealing, check in and go to bed when it's almost 2am.

When planning the trip we saw QPR would be playing Hull City at Loftus Road so we purchased tickets for that too. Before a game like this though, you definitely need some beer and so we go to the Central Bar, a Wetherspoon pub right off Shepherd's Bush station. This place is packed as usual, and we order some food and pints start flooding the table. Well, exactly that, because the waitress, poor her, she's getting driven crazy with all these gentlemen, especially the ones in white and blue, and she inadvertently knocks a couple of beers over my nephew Nicola. We all laugh while he's calling God names, and a few to the waitress to be honest, who simply disappears in the crowd. He looks like an old drunk who just wet his pants and of course we're taking the piss out of him.

After a good quarter of an hour under the hand drier he's more or less okay to go anyway.

So here we are at Loftus Road, which once was our home and I tell the boys of the spectre of a potential Fulham Park Rangers which, thank God, never happened.

We're sat just underneath the travelling fans, the game is quite entertaining and Hull win it 3-2 thanks to Bowen's brace. Happy time, QPHahahahaha.

On the way back we stop at another pub and then we spend the rest of the afternoon hanging around before having another pint at The Central. Incredibly, this time is Luca Z's turn to get some beer spilled over him! Did we do anything wrong or are the staff QPR supporters?!

At night, we end up in the Grand by Clapham Junction. It's perfect for the boys' age so we have a good time until an idiot randomly pulls my nephew's cap and laughs. The boys have circled it but we're not looking for trouble so I grab the guy's hand and show him the way saying, 'Keep going man, keep going.' He didn't look like the brightest creature on planet earth but it seems he got the message, we're all laughing and 'keep going' becomes historic.

It's been a good day. We grab a kebab to help the drinks soak while the boys are befriending a dreaded guy with green fingers.

It's already Sunday morning and even after a long night, to get fired up when you have to face Chelsea is a piece of cake. The midday kick-off means beer for breakfast. Well, almost. I know the Fulham Broadway area very well but my favourite place, Del Aziz, has closed down. What a pity. So we turn to the Cafè Nero at the corner. The staff are still almost all Italian, as it used to be when I was working nearby more than ten years ago. And I'm still amazed by the size choices of the beverages: half a litre of cappuccino would leave me shitting forever. Pardon my French.

Jeff texts me they're there so we meet up by the tube station. Again, it's like meeting someone from the family. Now the problem is where to drink in this 'Blue Area'. Mr Cook has joined us too and we opt for the Malt House in Farm Lane. We cheer on our new get-together and shortly after we're off to Stamford Bridge.

We're all gathered and getting in is super slow but we manage to reach our seats prior to kick-off.

It's an Italian affair here too as Chelsea's boss is the former Napoli manager Maurizio Sarri, and it's Italian cursing straight away when the boys give the ball away in their defensive half and Pedro swiftly puts the hosts in front. Four minutes on the clock. No comment.

The first half finishes and the score, thanks to Sergio Rico, stays the same. In the second half Fulham play much better against a far-from-pretty Chelsea. But we don't score and Ruben Loftus-Cheek, one of a very interesting breed of youngsters, puts the game to bed after a nice combination with

Hazard. Four thousand Fulham fans once again walk home empty-handed from the wrong side of Fulham Road.

Disappointed, we leave the ground towards the station and a little further down the street a Fulham artist expressed his talent on a white wall.

Memories pop up when passing the Barbarella Restaurant. It's now shut and it looks abandoned. What a pity. I'd be curious to know what has become of the owners. Jeff is waiting for us in an Aussie pub nearby. He didn't come to the game as there were not enough tickets so he gave us his.

This tells you once more what a great friend and person Jeff Slade is. I've tried a few times to tell him I'd give the game a miss and he could go but no chance. Thanks Jeff, you're just one of a kind, mate!

The pub is packed. It's not our kind of pub but more one of these modern, cold, lifeless ones. Anyway, the north London derby is on. The draft beer selection is poor, only piss lagers, but at least they've bottled ale.

Arsenal, after being 2-1 down at the interval, smack Spurs 4-2. They go fourth. We stay bottom, two points from safety and four from 14th place after 14 games.

We stay a little longer to enjoy our friends' company before going to Balham for food. Still sore from the defeat, on Monday morning Nicola and Manuel leave us to fly back to Italy while Luca Z, my nephew Nicola and myself will stay a few more days.

We're up and running in this late-December morning and have lunch at the Osteria Antica Bologna in Clapham, which is run by Umberto's best mate Marzio, who I know well from my days there. He was living with us in Tooting when I first came to London and he was the one who introduced us to the English breakfast in a little café around Tooting Broadway in the winter of 2000.

The food is great and it's like being in Italy. We're here because Alice, Umberto's only daughter, is now working here as a waitress. I'm so happy to see her after too long; she's now a beautiful girl with her mother's manners and style, and her father's inimitable smile.

She joins us at the pub after work and I must say my beloved friend would be so proud of his daughter because, beside being a wonderful person, she can down a pint! Being in her company is amazing and I'm over the moon. She's like a niece for me.

We then head north so Luca can see the Emirates and we pay tribute to the remains of the old Highbury.

Once back south of the river, we reunite in Balham with Mr Cook who takes us to a Turkish restaurant not far away. It's amazing food and a great time with another super friend.

It's Tuesday. For lunch we pay a visit to my friends Titta and Pier at their place, Farina and More, on Shepherd's Bush Road near Hammersmith. I haven't seen them for a while too so it's wonderful to meet again and I must say the place is perfect. We have lunch there and if you'll ever pass by give it a go because everything is homemade and delicious. They take good care of us.

After a few hugs, we're off to the Richmond, the closest pub, by the corner with Netherwood Road. They have pool tables and good draft ales. The place is empty, so even better. We spend the afternoon playing pool, drinking decent beer and chatting. I love this.

We leave after a couple of hours as we're going to West Ham v Cardiff at the London Stadium.

My nephews and friends want to see the other grounds in town, and of course we're hoping Cardiff get beaten.

The ground is soulless compared to Upton Park but it's still a good night out. The London Stadium is super modern, flash lights everywhere, the shop is big and there are plenty of people. We hope for lots of goals and a win for the Hammers so Cardiff will stay down.

Bubbles fly everywhere but the first half is far from bubbly. The second half is totally different and in just 12 minutes the result is sealed. Lucas Perez's brace and Michail Antonio's header see West Ham comfortably on top, and Josh Murphy's late goal is just a consolation.

Mission complete, Cardiff defeated, more good time in the capital; we can leave.

A couple of pints to celebrate and the night is over. Well, almost, as on the door of the hostel we meet a guy, a young carpenter from Wolverhampton who's smoking weed, and it seems Ealing eventually turned into the Notting Hill Carnival! He offers us some, taking out a bag that would make the *Top Boy* TV series look like *Teletubbies*. Even my room, located on the other flank, smells like it's been teleported to Jamaica.

Wednesday is our last day in London so we head north once again to check out Camden Town, which is buzzing as usual. It had lost it's magic for a few years and was run-down, with most stands only selling the same well-packed rubbish to make tourists think they had just bought a unique piece. But now it's on the up with street-food stalls, a rejuvenated spark and good vibes. We hang around, have a bite and then sit down for a pint and some chats. We're having a great time. After that we move to Putney, this time Jeff and Mark won't be with us so we grab some food in the Rocket, which is packed up with white colours. Time for another pint and off we go to the Cottage. Leicester await.

It's a vital home game and we really hope for a win. The lucky gates are used, of course.

The talk of the day is the reunion between Ranieri and the team he incredibly guided to Premier League glory just a couple of years ago. The Foxes look good but after Mitrović's wise play, Kamara puts us 1-0 up after fooling Çağlar Söyüncü. Joy! The second half has nothing much to offer. Cairney's hit goes begging just wide of the post, the sort of chance we have to take. Then, in the 74th minute, Shinji Okazaki's cross is well met by former Norwich star James Maddison. Totally unmarked, he taps in and a 1-1 scoreline now means 19 games in a row conceding goals.

We have to be happy with the point in the end but this is definitely not the way to stay up unfortunately. It's no surprise we're still bottom.

It's been an amazing time with my boys. I've seen friends, enjoyed food and beer; I leave my London with the bitter taste of the defeat at Stamford Bridge and even more of the points thrown away at the Cottage. It's going to be tough staying up, that's clear but, I'm Fulham 'til I die, so – come on you Whites!

On Thursday morning Nicola and Luca leave while I'll stay another day, moving to Balham for my last night. This gives me the opportunity to meet my dear friend Ben, a big Arsenal fan. We have lunch together and then I have an afternoon drink with Alice. A couple of hours of good talk and a little trip down memory lane. It's the same plan for the evening, this time with Mr Cook.

At least tomorrow I'll go back with my heart pampered by people I love.

Doomed

Soundtrack: 'Such A Shame' – Talk Talk

THE FOLLOWING two games are agony once again. It takes just 42 minutes for Manchester United to expose all our deficits with Ashley Young, Juan Mata and Romelu Lukaku easily putting the Red Devils 3-0 up. In the second half Kamara's second goal in a row gives us hope, quickly killed by Anguissa's red card. Marcus Rashford completes the rout late on. We concede two goals in less than half an hour the following week too when West Ham win 2-0 at the Cottage.

We come away with a point from Newcastle where we could have won it at the end and instead those minutes cost us again on Boxing Day against Wolves. One up thanks to Sessegnon's 74th-minute effort after missing a couple of glorious chances, we concede ten minutes later. Our defensive black-outs are costly and gift Saïss the easiest goal of his career.

But we finish on a high and the last game of the year is a thriller versus Huddersfield Town. Literally everything happens! We miss chances, so do Huddersfield, then Kamara wins a penalty but argues with Mitrović over who should take it. In the end it's the big Frenchman, who is honestly in fine form. But he misses it. And I bet all of us would like to kill him. Well, after Mitro, of course. Then, with almost the last kick of the game, Huddersfield throw away the chance to win it in a comic way. We counter, Sess's pass is perfect and our big Serbian puts the game to bed with Craven Cottage roaring. I don't know how my neighbours didn't call the police after all my shouting!

In the post-match interviews Ranieri says he wanted to kill Kamara. Well boss, take your place in the queue.

It's a vital win which can possibly mean a lot and also change the fate of the season as Huddersfield stay bottom while we climb up to 18th and Southampton, Cardiff, Newcastle and Palace are not that far away any more.

It's certainly good, unless you lose the first three games after the turn of the year! The away derby with Arsenal kicks off 2019 with a 4-1 defeat, where black sheep Kamara scores again. A few days later you'd look for an easy home win, and at least a little boost for the morale, but we end up losing 2-1 to Oldham Athletic in the FA Cup third round with Mitro missing a late penalty and the opponents scoring moments after. Oldham, a League Two club with a caretaker manager on the bench.

Then the sucker punch comes on 12 January anyway when after going in front with virtually the first kick of the match thanks to Schürrle, two own goals by Bryan and Odoi condemn us to defeat yet again, this time away at Burnley. These are not good signs at all.

A week later at the Cottage, it looks like somebody is taking the piss when Spurs striker Fernando Llorente scores an own goal. Dele Alli equalises at the beginning of the second half. We're not playing badly but when it's not your season you can see it clearly. The defence falls asleep and Winks heads in the winner for Spurs in the 93rd minute.

I switch off the TV, do the same with my laptop, go outside on the balcony and take a deep breath. January this year is glorious so I gather some friends and go out for a drink. If I'd stayed in I'd have smashed something for sure. These things happen when your fate seems already decided.

Former Liverpool winger and current Dutch international Ryan Babel signs for us from Turkish giants Beşiktaş. Is he going to be helpful in any way?

The next game sees the visit of Brighton to Craven Cottage. I have to work and I don't know if I prefer that or to watch the match. The first time I check, we're 2-0 down due to Murray's brace. I put the mobile back in disbelief. This pain is never-ending. But the second half is spirited and the game is overturned, 4-2 the final score. Chambers, who's incredibly proving to be our best signing, scores after just two minutes, Mitro bags a brace and even the misfiring Vietto finds joy. Safety is now two victories away. So what now? Hope? Reality? Dreams?

Norway utility man Håvard Nordtveit comes in on loan from Hoffenheim and winger Lazar Marković joins on a free from Liverpool while Stefan Johansen goes out on loan to West Brom and hothead Aboubakar Kamara to Yeni Malatyaspor.

Marković was a very interesting player a couple of seasons ago while Nordtveit can play in various roles, so let's see what they can add.

Unfortunately for the month of February the answer is nothing. Four defeats in four games mean relegation is almost certain.

Palace complete the double by beating us 2-0 with goals from Milivojević and Schlupp before United come and thrash us 3-0 at home with Pogba getting two and Martial completing the rout. Babel scores his first goal with just three minutes on the clock at the London Stadium and I hope we left some good luck there on our visit but no, West Ham score three and take the points. Two first-half goals from Southampton see us off at St Mary's on the last game of this awful month.

This is enough to demonstrate Ranieri was just another mistake of this badly planned season and the Tinkerman is replaced by our former captain Scott Parker.

If February was painful, March is possibly worse because it starts with a 2-1 home defeat in the derby with the Blues where even Gonzalo Higuaín manages to score for Chelsea. Leicester slap us 3-1 with Vardy's brace winning it for the Foxes. Our fall towards the Championship continues with Liverpool taking all three points in London, Babel equalising with the classic ex-player goal only to be cancelled out by Milner's late penalty. All these games are like a knife constantly pushed further down into our hearts.

Manchester City also win 2-0 at Craven Cottage, 27 minutes of sweat enough to win the game.

April arrives and even Watford thrash us, 4-1, which is a very hard lesson to swallow. Babel is again on the score sheet and I have to hold my hands up because I really didn't believe he'd do so well. I simply thought he was coming back to the Premier League to pocket some good money and play in the best league in the world once again. But I was wrong and I wish he'd come at the beginning of the season instead of somebody else.

This game marks our immediate return to the Championship after just a season and a £100m transfer campaign. Quite a lot of people say it's better like that, the Championship is more fun and blah, blah, blah.

I definitely don't think so. We're Fulham for fuck's sake! Not even a decade ago we were in a European final and since then we've already been relegated twice. Fair enough, we showed we were not up to the standard, but I can name at least three other clubs who are not better than us and stayed up.

And the Ranieri appointment, what went through the owners' heads? It was a panic decision from people who don't seem to know what they're doing. They had the money, they bought a toy and then realised they didn't know how to play with it.

But you're playing with our faith, our love, our Fulham FC.

Of the remaining five games we even win three in a row without conceding a goal, before losing two without scoring one. But yes, this is already another story.

One More Time

Soundtrack: 'Get Up, Stand Up' – Bob Marley

THE SUMMER of 2019 is a great one of work where we provide the catering for Borussia Dortmund's centre-back Manuel Akanji's wedding. Germany superstar Marco Reus and English next big thing Jadon Sancho are among the guests and the latter shows great professionalism even at this young age.

My nephews make me super happy when they decide to spend their holidays in Mallorca for the second year running. Manuel and the two Nicolas are accompanied by Andrea, another one of their friends.

The week in their company is amazingly fun even if it's quite tough to cope with them. I'm not that young any more!

Fulham is often the centre of our talks but when they ask for a forecast I'm stuck. After many years of optimism and hope this time I don't want to get exposed or say anything. I'll get behind the boys, that's for sure, but I honestly don't know what to expect.

Scott Parker is a well-respected person, he looks like a wise man with a strong will. But he has no managerial experience beyond those handful of games he was in charge of a couple of months ago.

Maybe it's me being a little negative this time around but even our kits look cheap and chosen without enthusiasm. Our home one is very simple, almost 100 per cent white with some red and black details. Our away one is once again red with fading black/grey stripes. You can find exactly the same Adidas T-shirt online for less than a tenner.

Going down means again all out and all in but the very good news is that our big man sticks with the cause. Mitrović will play with us in the Championship and that is something to really cheer for in my opinion.

Josh Onomah comes in from Spurs, while the main business is again done with loans. A player I liked a lot last time here, Portuguese winger Ivan Cavaleiro, is signed from Wolves while another wide player, Frenchman Anthony Knockaert, joins from Brighton.

Harry Arter's long-rumoured transfer eventually materialises in August, a month when we also sign midfielder Harrison Reed from Southampton and his almost namesake Bobby Decordova-Reid comes in from Cardiff. Five potentially cracking loanees.

Big-money purchases Seri and Anguissa have already departed, again on loan, to Galatasaray and Villarreal.

All pundits name Fulham as promotion favourites but Barnsley, a newly promoted side from League One, beat us 1-0 in the opening game. And then we win three in a row! Blackburn are beaten 2-0 in London and Huddersfield 2-1 in Yorkshire. Cairney and Mitro secure the first three points, Mitro and Cavaleiro the second.

The 4-0 display in the home win over Millwall is the one to catch the eye though. Amazing football and three goals in the first 32 minutes. Were the visitors too bad or did Fulham show what they're capable of?

It's a doubt that will stay with us for a while as we then only get one point from the remaining two fixtures of the month.

Just three days after the Millwall game we lose 2-1 at Craven Cottage to Lewis Grabban and his Nottingham Forest team-mates, with Mitro continuing his scoring form. Then we draw 1-1 at Cardiff, with our Serbian forward bagging his fifth goal in these six games.

September has an international break so our next game is on the 14th. I incredibly managed to get holidays at work and so I got a ticket to Buenos Aires. Months ago I met an Argentine girl in Palma and we hooked up. I've always wanted to visit South America so here I am.

The capital is huge and all my friends have warned me about not going around with my mobile in sight and to be always careful. The days there are amazing and with Julia there's a big crush. Shit.

Unfortunately there are no league games but I manage to visit the famous Boca Juniors ground La Bombonera and then I find out there's a cup game not far away. Lanús, a team I know and follow from time to time due to a friend who used to come to support Vicenza but is originally from there, will play Argentinos Juniors at the Arsenal Sarandí stadium.

I ask the taxi driver my girl recommended me and he says it's a dodgy area so I should just go there for the game then don't hang around or look too unfamiliar, jump in a taxi and leave.

I book an Uber which is quite popular here and super cheap for me due to the exchange rate and he says the same. 'I'll leave you close to the ground, go straight there, watch the game and leave.'

I must say I've never felt too uncomfortable in my life, nor in Milan, nor in London but here, I'd have love to be here with a friend at least. Anyway, here I am, quite dressed down in all black. I buy the ticket in the Lanus end and I like that here you can still put up banners and flags, and hardcore fans have drums and flares. I love it! When chants go on I pretend I'm singing. I speak fluent Spanish but here it's another, completely different world.

The supporters are immense. They don't stop encouraging their team, and sing and shout relentlessly. Fair play to them.

Lanús win 3-1. Maybe I brought good luck! As police let us leave it's dark, I keep my hands in my pockets, look nowhere and quickly reach the shopping centre nearby where my Uber should arrive soon.

Nothing weird happens but you can tell just what the area is like. Argentina is unfortunately a very dangerous country due to the financial crises that too often hit this otherwise marvellous place. Many Argentines have Italian roots so I feel for them.

When club football resumes for Fulham it's another 1-1 draw, this time in London where West Brom get their point in the 80th minute after new signing Knockaert has scored his second in four games. And we concede very late once again in the following away match, at Sheffield Wednesday, with the Owls' equaliser for 1-1 coming in the 93rd minute. Damn.

Wigan are next under the floodlights of Craven Cottage and an easy 2-0 sees us returning to winning days as September ends with us in seventh place.

It's been a long month work-wise as it's probably the best period of the year to get married, which means a lot of events for the company I work for. I'm pleased and it's entertaining. I made some great friendships which is never easy with colleagues but together with Argentinians Mariano, Manu, Maxi, Marcelo and Pablo, and Uruguayan Sebastian, we've formed a very nice group of mates. Our *asados*, the Argentine way to call a barbecue or our ever-entertaining nights out, are becoming memorable. Palma is fun and there's plenty to do. On Tuesday there's La Ruta Martiana, which can be translated into The Tuesday Crawl, where you go from bar to bar downtown enjoying little tapas and a *caña*, the equivalent of a small beer.

This is usually what participants remember; the second part of the night remains a faded memory.

Five games in October will help us see where we stand. The beginning is encouraging, a 4-1 victory at Reading with the boys three goals up after just 29 minutes. Cairney hits the opener then Mitro two, and our captain will also score the fourth.

Charlton at home should be another three-pointer but no, they go in front twice only for Cavaleiro and Mitro to earn us a point.

After another international break we resume our campaign with a bad 2-0 defeat at Stoke. Four days later Fulham bounce back immediately with a tougher than expected victory, a 3-2 home defeat of Luton Town. Mitro scores a hat-trick and is our true love.

The month is closed with a disappointing 0-0 away draw at struggling Middlesbrough where new first-choice goalkeeper Rodak is sent off after only 17 minutes. It's a little dip in form maybe, because we're then trashed 3-0 at home by Hull City and my birthday is down the toilet.

But the boys have some pride and that, linked with class, brings four wins in a row. Our top scorer's effort is enough for a 1-0 win in Birmingham, so it's a pity our next game will only take place in 12 days.

The good point is, I'm going to be there! Well, just.

Is It Really Just a Game?

Soundtrack: 'Born Slippy' – Underworld

OUR HOME derby versus QPR is originally planned for Saturday, 23 October, and with the boys we've already arranged our trip. We'll fly into London on Friday night and then meet up with Jeff and Mark for the game the following day. Then it's announced that the game has been moved to be broadcast live on TV. WTF?!

I have to tell you that I'm quite tired of this TV-rights tyranny where we supporters always come last. It's disrespectful to say the least.

I'm lucky enough that I can change my flight and without breaking the bank. The boys unfortunately cannot as they have work to do and can't alter their holiday plan again. Of course we're all disappointed. A home derby, even a Championship one, is always a game you look forward to a little more than others so having to change everything so very late is awful.

I leave the flat and get the bus as I like to be at the airport early. I don't like surprises. I'm relaxed but decide to double-check the flight time. Shit, it's 11.07am and the flight is at midday. I'll never make it. I jump down at the first stop leaving the bus driver puzzled. I'm looking for a taxi as the airport is just 15 minutes away by car but there's no sign of one when you really need it!

Eventually one arrives and I get in, explaining I'm in a rush and telling the story. He understands but drives as if he was taking a group of pensioners on a tour around the island.

When we reach the airport I run, beating every world record of sprinting with luggage! Security control is luckily fast and I restart my personal Olympics of running, jumping and dribbling past other travellers before eventually reaching the check-in. God, I made it, I can breathe again.

I board the plane second to last with my face still red. I'm alive and on my way to London.

As I had to change flight and land in Gatwick I've texted Rachel, Paolo's former girlfriend. She works for the environmental department of the airport and we meet up after a long time. With a pint of Abbot in our hands we go back in time updating each other about our lives.

This time me and the boys are staying in Earl's Court, which is spot-on logistics-wise. I check into the hostel and find a room that is basic but very clean. I leave my luggage, get my Fulham scarf on, plus the promotion black kit, and hit the road.

I have a strange feeling that I've already been here but my mind is set for the game so I move on.

The Rocket is getting full and with Mark we have to adapt to the little shelf by the column. Doom Bar at £2.39 and Abbot at £2.59 means heaven is a place on earth. Still Mark manages to drink a cider, God forgive him.

We move to Craven Cottage and I instantaneously feel at home. There's not a full house and it's a pity. Hugill's early goal is levelled and then overturned by a rare Kamara brace. The big Frenchman might be proving his worth in this league.

I take a video of the jubilant crowd and send it to the boys. I'm very happy that we've put one over QPHahahaha once more and so when they eventually arrive by Uber from the airport, the first round is on me!

But it's not going to be a crazy night for us as tomorrow we'll get up early because we're heading to Brighton for their game with Leicester.

I like Brighton. I have some fond memories there with Paolo, Julian and some other friends when quite a few years earlier we went down for a fish and chips on the beach.

I got in touch with my former colleague Viviana, whom I worked with in the military base in Vicenza a long time ago. She lives in Brighton now so we catch up. I've asked her and some other friends for a recommendation over the best fish and chips place and the choice is Bankers. The internet confirms it so there we go.

We're the very first customers as it's quite early but the kick-off is at 3pm so we have to be in quickly. The claim of the place should be 'size doesn't matter' as we order the medium portion but what we get is more similar to a whale than a haddock!

The award they received was well deserved as the food is really good, tasty and not greasy. The only down point is they haven't got draft beer so we have to settle for bottled Sussex Best. A good bitter anyway, I must add.

With happy bellies we head to the train station where we join the crowd towards the Amex Stadium. Another ground on the list.

The game is nothing special, like today's weather. The first half is quite boring but the second is more animated and Leicester City's famous counter-attack eventually manages to tear the home defence apart. Perez opens the scoring before Vardy seals it from the penalty spot.

We get back to town and head to a pub for a much-needed pint. Fun is clearly the focal point and we definitely go for it.

We wave goodbye to Viviana and jump on the train back to London, heading to Balham where the boys want to go back to the Turkish restaurant Mr Cook took us to on our last visit.

Unfortunately he won't be with us this time as he's away. This saddens me a little because he's a dear friend and I won't be going to see either him or Jeff this time.

Anyway, when I try to book, the girl says to go back around nine because they're packed. I make it clear to keep a table for us as they won't be disappointed, and then leave. The Devonshire is close by so we sit outside, some of the boys can smoke and we can all have a good pint of mixed.

This time, beside myself and the usual crew of Manuel, Nicola, Nicola Z and Luca Zoppi, Lorenzo also joins us. He's their team-mate at football and a big football boy.

After some malty heaven I quickly stop by Sainsbury's for some wine. The Turks don't sell alcohol, and here we are ordering some food from the Middle East. I definitely recommend the Pasha Mangal in Bedford Hill – it's simply great.

The waitress looks happy we got back and at the same time she's amazed by the quantity of food we're devouring. We surely contributed to a very successful night for the place.

Stuffed like a Scotch egg, Manuel and I head back to the hostel while the others stay in Balham for a gin and tonic. Good boys.

It's Sunday and we couldn't manage to get tickets for a game so we're going to have lunch somewhere and take it from there.

Close by the hostel there are quite a few pubs and we get a table in the Courtfield. We haven't planned much so we take it easy – a nice meal, some beer, a typical chill-out Sunday. Or so we thought.

Firstly, we hear somebody speaking Italian. Not such a surprise in London, you might say, so we turn and see three guys talking. One is wearing a Verona jersey. Verona, for us from Vicenza, are like Chelsea for a Fulham fan.

I quickly go back to the hostel and make an emphatic return proudly wearing the brand new Vicenza home shirt the boys got me for my birthday. The *Veronesi* get it, finish their beer and leave.

We don't care who goes though, because, punctual as if he was Swiss, my dear friend Mark shows up in the pub. It's hugs time and the beginning of the end.

Pints of ale start flooding the table, followed by the 'finger game', where every participant puts a finger on the glass and takes a turn at guessing how many fingers will still be there after his guess; the main culprit of our behaviour's downfall. At the table next to us three ladies are celebrating a birthday and start chatting us up. Unfortunately the birthday woman thinks it's her lucky day and once up, she whispers to my ear that she's going to the toilet. Sorry … you haven't won, my dear. I don't want to be rude but she was not the most gifted girl looks-wise. I report to the boys what she said and we all have a big laugh. She comes back and doesn't look too annoyed about it. Good girl.

Our drinking pace is worrying and I reckon there's a waiter only attending our table because empty glasses are quickly swapped for full ones.

It's dark when somebody from the staff tells us they got some complaints about our noise.

We're having so much fun, I understand we're a bit loud but jeez, we're not in church and we're not molesting other tables or making a mess, just having a laugh and drinking beer.

After another waitress comes to us about the same topic we decide to leave. We made your day, Courtfield pub.

It's almost 8pm and as tipsy as ever we hit the road in search of another public house when we bump into KFC.

As I said before, I'm for a healthy regime. I eat good food, I don't smoke, but I have two vices I can't resist: Kentucky Fried Chicken and M&M's, the peanut ones.

So every time I come to London I always have KFC a few times. We have it in Mallorca too but the Spanish recipe is different and not good at all. I jump into it and manage to get some food before finding the pub for us where they're also showing Sheffield United v Manchester United.

We get a table at the Earls Court Tavern and keep on enjoying good pints of British ale properly accompanied by some bags of crisps. Salt and vinegar for me please.

It's binge drinking at its best but it's such a great day that ends up again in KFC. They're closing, it's late so we have to be happy with the little they have left. We hit the road again, and hilarious pictures and videos of that night still pop up in our WhatsApp chat from time to time. It seems the count calls for 20 pints per head. Plus various shots for the unlucky losers of the finger game.

Luca crashes on his bed still completely dressed while we all fall in a deep sleep almost immediately. The pints count is adjusted to 21 but it could possibly be higher.

Monday morning could be easier but it could definitely be much, much worse. I get a text from Mark. 'I hardly remember anything from yesterday.' That says a lot.

As we get back to life, tales from the day before come up and we can't stop laughing. We hit the road and here's the revelation: in a flash I remember that Umberto used to live perfectly next to the hostel. Wow, I remember facing the little garden from his window having a beer or sharing a joint. Good old days.

With my head still down memory lane we reach King's Cross as we're going to travel to the Midlands for Aston Villa v Newcastle. To get tickets I created six different email addresses because I could not purchase six tickets in one go. We're going to be a little split up but it won't bother us much.

When we get to Birmingham we find a good pub just across the road. The beer served is good and the Toon Army are present. And of course they're in their shirts – no jackets or coats.

A couple of pints later we're on our way to another historical place in the football world. Of course I'm still remembering the play-off final when we left Mr Terry in tears but tonight I'm here as a neutral just to hopefully enjoy a good game.

Villa Park is a ground I like. It's a proper British stadium and we were all looking forward to today. In the end we manage to sit all within metres of each other among 40,000 other spectators. The game is not impressive and quite boring to be honest then in four minutes we see two goals, Irishman Hourihane scoring a brilliant free kick and assisting El Ghazi for the second. At least the atmosphere is okay but on the pitch there's really not much to entertain us. Newcastle are quite poor to be honest.

It ends 2-0 to the Villans so we rush to the station and manage to squeeze into the second packed train which takes us back to Birmingham where we'll get another one towards London.

It's been a long but good day, another ground on our map, some nice time together with my nephews and their friends. We crash on the seats, some of us having a little nap, some with their phones, a little chat here and there, until somebody from the same coach starts yelling and singing loud. You can easily tell they're drunk.

This goes on for too long. A father with his son is quite annoyed as the boy is moaning he can't sleep. After a while, Lorenzo shouts 'basta' which means stop it in Italian. The dick mumbles something, gives some rest to our tired ears for a time then starts all over again.

A couple of us remind him that the people have had enough. He gets up and menacingly confronts Lorenzo, who's got a temper for himself. Nicola Z quickly jumps up, as does the asshole's friend, and the air is suddenly electric. Then maybe the two clowns realise it would be two v six so they calm down.

The bigger one, a quite stocky but average-height Irishman, becomes friendly and starts talking to the boys. 'Sorry, I'm drrrrrunk' is the apology.

Accepted. There he goes on talking about his life, with a girl somewhere taking care of his son and telling us he's a former boxer who never lost a match.

Nicola Z makes the critical question, 'How many matches did you fight?'

'Three.'

Okay. God bless you.

We arrive at King's Cross, it's night time, we get a taxi and we're back in Earl's Court. It takes us half an hour to finally sleep because every now and again one of us breaks the silence improvising a 'sorry I'm drrrrrunk' in a weird Irish accent. Good night.

When we wake up on the Tuesday morning the laughing restarts while we get ready for another hopefully great day. Tonight is Craven Cottage time! All together again and we can't wait any longer.

We have a quick breakfast at the Pret a Manger by the Earl's Court station before getting the tube to Hammersmith. A walk on Shepherd's Bush Road and we're back at Farina and More, the restaurant of my friends Titta and Pier. As usual they greet us in a lovely way while we take a seat. Two plates of Italian charcuterie and *gnocco fritto* (something similar to pieces of fried dough) as big as a UFO land on our table.

The lads are in their 20s and the voracity is amazing. After devouring the starter, huge portions of homemade pasta arrive. God, are we on *Man v. Food*?

Stuffed as pigs we thank Titta, Pier and their staff and roll over outside, slowly reaching the Richmond. Yes, we like our spots.

It's a cool afternoon once more. The boys know a couple of guys from our home town who now live in London and they've invited them to the game. The Fulham family keeps growing.

Luca and Richard join us at the pub where the ale is already taking care of our bellies. But it's time to live, the Rocket is waiting for us. Putney is buzzing when we get there and the Rocket is packed. Mark has also joined us and the pre-match ritual is in place.

I leave the boys behind because I hate missing the kick-off. Derby County have lost three in a row so it could be tricky, but just seven minutes into the game Bobby Decordova-Reid opens his Fulham account. There's still no sign of the boys but Fulham are dominating, and when they eventually show up they are quite tipsy.

We're on the very first row of seats behind the goal and Lorenzo, who's never been to a match here but is a big Vicenza fan, is impressed.

In the 40th minute Mitrović makes it 2-0 to virtually confirm our third win on the spin and party time keeps going.

Kamara looks another player and maybe being arrested helped him cool his temper. Wayne Rooney will soon join the Rams but I hope for him he's not watching this.

The second half is the same story. Fulham should score more but we have to wait until the 89th minute for our captain Tom Cairney to put the game to bed with the third goal. Lorenzo, helped by the fumes of alcohol, jumps over the boards and before reaching the pitch he's guarded out by the stewards. No comment.

The game ends in victory and I'm extremely happy. I want us to go straight back up to the Premier League.

We leave the always beautiful Craven Cottage and meet Lorenzo just outside the gates. Thankfully the stewards saw he was harmless and let him go.

The till of the stadium shop is an infinite sequence of beeps with supporters pumping cash into the club of their hearts. We're no different and a few shirts and other items will fly back to Italy and Mallorca with us.

There's still just about time for a last drink at the Rocket so we enter the place in hope. Yes, we can be served, but it's last orders. I hit the toilet and once out I see the boys carrying three or four glasses each. My God.

We sit down putting a few tables together while the pub is getting empty.

Some pints are not drinkable. They got us the very last drops of the barrel. The manager writes me a voucher on the back of their business card and basically kick us out. Understandable, but what a pity.

The fresh breeze of London hits our faces and while happy and drunk we salute each other, Luca wearing Fulham's home kit on top of his sweater still with the tags on. Hopefully he'll get home sooner or later.

Wednesday has come and it means only one thing, the end of another incredible adventure in London.

We have lunch together; a nice pie in Earl's Court accompanied by a good pint is the right way to say goodbye.

The boys leave for Stansted and I get the tube towards Bayswater where I'll stay some more days. Luca sends us a picture. He just woke up, wearing the Fulham shirt. Still with the tags.

Julia is flying to Europe and we spend some lovely days as Mitro's brace in Swansea helps Fulham clinch a fourth win in a row. What an amazing month November has eventually turned out to be.

Well, apart from the 30th.

I decide to take Julia to one of my favourite spots in London, Borough Market. When we get there it's packed with police, a helicopter watching from the sky, and we smell that something isn't right. The policeman Julia asks for news says nothing so we enter the market. It's packed as usual and visitors seem relaxed, until the moment we hear somebody screaming and in a second, hundreds of people are running crazily towards us. Someone is screaming 'run', someone else 'oh my God', and people are crying. I grab Julia's hand and run towards the exit, perhaps not the safest choice but everybody is coming from the other way so there aren't many options.

Once outside police are shouting 'leave that way' so we follow, running without asking many questions until we felt far enough to stop. Ghosts of the bombing days back in 2005 hit me but we heard nothing.

In the end we'd find out that one guy attacked wayfarers with a knife over London Bridge and that panic erupted in the market when people heard the police shootings.

Well, it's behind us now but every time there's an attack to my beloved London my heart gets punched heavily.

Julia goes back to Argentina and I've got a feeling I won't see her any more. Mark comes and picks me up; some friends are in town so he wants me to join them and that's the best thing that could happen today.

2020

Soundtrack: 'Do You Really Want to Hurt Me' – Culture Club

WELL, WELL, well. I'm still thinking about the wonderful ten days I've spent in London, full of love, football and beer when the first two weeks of December slap me straight in the face.

Bristol City win 2-1 at the Cottage on 7 December and just three days later it's 2-1 again, usually our lucky score, but this time high-flying Preston beat us. Maguire puts them one up then Rafferty gets sent off which means we're going to play the entire second half 11 v ten. Incredibly though, Nugent scores a second for the home side and Mitrović's late goal is not enough to get anything out of the game. Four days on and Brentford have the last word in the west London derby with a 1-0 and a third straight defeat for us. Wow, what happened to the incredible Fulham we saw in November?

I'm baffled and the boys are too as they keep texting me because they cannot believe it either.

On 21 December we welcome Leeds United, unbeaten in 11 and second in the table. It's redemption time and this time the 2-1 score is in our favour. Mitro from the spot nets his 17th of the campaign, Bamford levels in the second half but in the 69th minute Josh Onomah shows why he is in the England under-21s. His drive is a bullet that Kiko Casilla cannot save. We're back in third place, nine points adrift of our Yorkshire opponents.

I'm home for Christmas and as usual I'm loving it. A big lunch all together and Mum's lasagne is always yummy. Later on, Luca and Nicola show up to wrap up the celebrations.

On Boxing Day Fulham make the short trip to Luton for a festive rollercoaster. It's 3-3 at Kenilworth Road – 1-1 within nine minutes and 2-1 to the Hatters at the interval. Mitro levels, Cornick thinks he has just won it for Luton in the 84th minute only for Bobby Decordova-Reid to level deep in injury time.

It's a comeback that gives a morale boost and on the back of that Fulham edge a 1-0 win over Stoke in the last game of the decade, Decordova-Reid again scoring the goal.

So 12 points in four games then none in three followed by seven in three. The Whites definitely are not a team of half measures.

I'm back in Mallorca as I got a well-paid job for New Year's Eve. I'll be home in the early hours but I should be okay to watch Fulham take on Reading in the afternoon.

It would have been better to stay in bed though as Reading are 2-0 up early in the second half and Cavaleiro's effort in the second is not enough to improve the unbeaten run.

A word is spreading that a new virus, similar to flu, has hit Europe after infecting many people in China.

Ten days after the home debacle, Fulham are back at the KCOM Stadium where this time Cav's goal is more than enough for the three points. A week later comes another 1-0 win, this time on home soil over Middlesbrough thanks to a fine Knockaert goal.

The short trip to Charlton earns the boys a point but it feels like two points lost. A win would have seen us within just one point of automatic promotion but it was not meant to be. January goes with two wins, one draw and one loss.

February kicks in and the news reports say this virus called Covid-19 is causing havoc around the world and fears of a pandemic are growing. The press are really pushing it.

Life goes on and so does football and Fulham open the month with an entertaining 3-2 home win over Huddersfield Town. The first half is pure show as the Cottagers go 3-0 up with an amazing display of stylish football. Decordova-Reid, Cairney and Mitro are on the score sheet in a game that looks defined already in the 31st minute. Emile Smith Rowe, a very interesting prospect on loan from Arsenal, and Steve Mounié get two in just four minutes and with six minutes to go to the break the score is 3-2. That will be the final result thanks to another good performance by Rodak, who is now the first choice in goal. We're still flirting with promotion while the Terriers are in danger of relegation.

On 8 February, Mitrović scores his 20th league goal and Fulham win 1-0 at Ewood Park but the news is we're now level on points with Leeds. Automatic promotion is more than just a dream.

But the Championship is a tough league and we all know it well, we've learned it the hard way in the past few years, and Millwall first and Barnsley after are there to remind that to us.

Mitrović is loving his football and scores at The Den with just three minutes on the clock but it's a proper case of waking up the sleepy lion as the hosts fight back immediately. Böðvarsson equalises five minutes later and we only have to thank the bar for Wallace not overturning it from the spot. The same bar we'll curse in stoppage time when Kebano could have won it for us.

Two days later the worst game of the season sees us lose 3-0 at home to Barnsley, a team deep in the relegation zone. Cauley Woodrow has the last laugh over his former employers.

It's a mess from which we kind of recover a week later at Derby. Wayne Rooney shows he still has it with a penalty but Mitrović responds well and it's 1-1, back putting points on the table. We need more though if we're to keep fighting for the automatic promotion.

Up to the 88th minute at home to Swansea it doesn't seem we got the message anyway. Then Kebano is fouled inside the box and I jump from the sofa where I'm sat watching the game.

Mitro takes the ball and I reckon I'm not the only one already celebrating the victory. But no, he misses it. Swansea's goalkeeper saves an unusually weak penalty from the big Serbian. Unbelievable. I crash back on the sofa powerless.

Fair play to the boys as they keep on pushing and Mitro redeems himself with a fine header from Kamara's good cross in the 90th minute. I jump again, this time spilling the beer I had left on the table after the missed opportunity. Texts flow in from the WhatsApp chat with the nephews.

A few days later, Preston come to Craven Cottage and revenge is swiftly served with a good 2-0 win. Nugent, who sealed our defeat in the first game, scores an incredible own goal doubled by Kamara with the last kick of the match. Six points on the spin and dream mode on once more.

I fly home in a very good mood. I'm going to spend some time with family and we'll celebrate my mum's 83rd birthday together. Some friends are warning me that news reports in Italy are not good about this damn virus and Lombardy, where the airport I'm flying to is located, has been badly hit by Covid.

I honestly don't know what to think. I don't watch TV, especially the news, and try to keep myself up to date using various channels of information and this thing really smells rotten to me. Anyway, let's see what happens. Once landed

I'll go straight to the desk for the rental car and head off to Vicenza.

Bristol City prove a tough nut to crack for us this season and we come back from Ashton Gate with only a point, needing Cairney's late goal for it.

The night before, I met Lara for the first time. She's from Vicenza too, just a 15-minute drive from the village where I was born. We started chatting from time to time on Facebook and decided to meet on Friday, 6 March, once I booked my flight. We have friends in common but never really met each other. I'm curious.

We have dinner together and it's a pleasant night. I like her and we plan to get out again before I go back to Palma.

Well, it's going to be a while until that day it seems as the Italian government decides to shut shop and we enter confinement. It's surreal. After 15 years away I find myself obligated to stay here in Mossano. My home town. My mum just turned 83 so I'm pleased I'll have to spend time with her at least. The weather is gorgeous and I rediscover this place and the neighbourhood. I can go to the supermarket and now the two councils of Mossano and Barbarano are merged, I can take a longer route home as the law allows you to move freely within your area of residence.

A lot of football leagues around the world are on hold and very few games are played. Fulham stay third in the Championship while Covid hits the entire planet. Mental.

I spend my time reading and writing, helping Mum here and there and, as a good Italian, cooking. I consider myself very lucky to be here and not confined in a small flat. We've got a garden and we're in the countryside so no traffic at all, clean air, silence.

Lara and I are chatting on WhatsApp regularly especially after my return flight got cancelled. What on earth is going on?!

March is gone with another flight booked and then cancelled, Ryanair and Volotea both refunding quickly. I have to stay here and nobody knows until when because it's general chaos it seems. In Mallorca it's the same and they've been confined too.

I can't remember when I was last home for Easter and now I am we can't go out. I haven't seen my childhood friends so far. I can tell people are getting mad because this limitation of freedom is absurd.

April is nearly finished and the most exciting thing of the week is Friday when I usually go to the supermarket. Some people are wearing masks and you should disinfect your hands before entering it. Are we in a movie?

At least it seems that from 6 May people will be allowed to visit their partners if they do not live together. Eventually, I manage to see Lara again. I think there could be something between us.

Before coming home I stopped working for the catering company. I didn't want to go back but was open to a meeting to listen to their plans. With a little surprise they told me they no longer needed me as a maître as our views were different. I was very happy at the same time because leaving would not have given me the exit bonus I'm instead entitled to now. Yeah baby.

I'm seeing Lara a lot as she's still home too so I have mixed feelings when flights are resumed and I can book mine for 8 June. Although this time has helped to make my mind up. I'll come back to Italy for good. I was already considering if I wanted to stay in Mallorca and have my life there forever or move somewhere else. Back to Vicenza is definitely an option.

I also considered moving to Argentina as I was really in love with Julia, but Covid and some other personal matters did the rest.

Bergamo's airport is almost empty. I've never seen it like this. I'm used to a crowded and busy terminal while this time you could hear the echo of your voice if you screamed. Also the flight is so unusual, just a few masked passengers. Surreal, this is the word. Again.

Really?

Soundtrack: 'History Repeating'
– The Propellerheads

PALMA LOOKS like the set of an apocalypse-centred disaster movie. The buzzing area I'm used to has been replaced by a decadent, sad bunch of streets with just a few people around, all restaurants are closed and people go around looking at the floor. It scares me a little and I'm expecting tumbleweeds any time soon.

I catch up with my friends, whom I've been missing a lot, and they update me on the last news. The good thing is that Luigi, my friend and former employer, needs a hand tonight at the restaurant as at night time there are still some people around.

In the end we strike a deal and I'll be back working at Bunker's. He knows I'll leave within months and that Lara will come to visit me in early August. Hopefully there will be no other confinements or closures in the meantime.

The Championship resumes too but it couldn't go worse for Fulham as we lose the first game 2-0 to local rivals Brentford when I watch and where we concede in the 88th and 91st minutes. Craven Cottage is completely empty due to the new Covid regulations and the view, not only on the pitch, is scary and extremely sad.

A week after we're well beaten once more, 3-0 by Leeds at Elland Road, and I wish the league didn't resume if it had to go like this. Leeds make it six wins in a row including the results they had before the break. We're fourth and Mitro will probably be banned afterwards. What's going on for Christ's sake?

Then, when you think it's all gone, your confidence is low and all your dreams are almost shattered, there's always QPHAHAHA to cheer you up! At Loftus Road, now rebranded the Kiyan Prince Foundation Stadium, there's a victory for Fulham once more.

Hugill scores early again, this time almost with the first kick of the game, but Arter, whose resilience and fighting spirit are proving vital for us, levels 20 minutes later and then the unexpected hero Cyrus Christie smashes in the winner in the 75th minute. What a nice number (it's the year I was born in). Fulham are back to winning days and celebrating our American legacy four days later, on 4 July, by beating Birmingham City 1-0 at the Cottage. Onomah gets all fans screaming in front of their TVs, phones or computers on the 95th minute.

Just three days on, Fulham go north to Nottingham Forest for a third win in a row thanks to Arter's belter from way outside the box. And it's a massive win over a potential play-off rival.

We now welcome Cardiff for the fourth game in ten days. The suspension of the league has affected the calendar so now games will come in a hectic schedule.

The Cottagers have recovered from a tough June and with Mitro and Onomah they inflict a 2-0 punishment to the Bluebirds. Automatic promotion is in sight, even if it's not going to be easy.

On 14 July Fulham travel to The Hawthorns to face second-placed West Brom. It's a nervy encounter that finishes 0-0, probably ending our hopes of going up in second.

It seems it didn't dent the morale though as a hectic home game versus Sheffield Wednesday sees Fulham win 5-3. Kebano and a brace from Mitrović get the Whites 3-0 up in the first half with our little wizard restoring the three-goal lead in the second half after Nuhiu had scored for the visitors. Far from considering themselves beaten, the Owls scored two more goals with Murphy and again Nuhiu before Bobby Decordova-Reid scored another of his ever important point-winner goals. What a game!

This incredibly means our hopes are alive ahead of the last game of the regular season, which will see us travelling to Wigan. Leeds can already celebrate as they're the 2019/20 Championship winners.

Unfortunately at the DW Stadium it's just 1-1 but even a win would have not been enough for us. There's a worse fate for Wigan though. They're relegated, even if confirmation will only come after the result of their appeal against the massive 12-point deduction suffered.

It's the play-offs again, the second time in three years. Will our coronary arteries bear all this? And there's no time to rest on our laurels as only five days later Fulham are back in action at the Cardiff City Stadium where the Bluebirds, our relegation companions only last season, are going to fight for promotion with us.

It's a shame and a pain that such a game is played in an empty stadium but mind you, no team will view this match as less important as a result.

I'm at the Lennox, my lucky pub, with almost nobody around as tourism has terribly decreased after many governments considered Spain a dangerous destination.

I was initially annoyed that Mitrović could not make it. He's the league's leading scorer and a player of pivotal importance in our game. But the boys step up once more and put in an immense display of almost total annihilation.

Cairney hits the post before Onomah improvises a skiing slalom inside Cardiff's box. It looks like he has moved into a liquid state and floats among the rival defenders as if they were stones. Kebano completes the artistic win with a masterpiece free kick.

A 2-0 win for Fulham means a spot in the final is almost secured. Don't let down the guard though boys, please.

Three days later I'm unfortunately at work but clearly my mind and my heart are somewhere else. I don't resist, I grab the phone and run to the toilet and read that it's 1-1, Kebano scoring again. Come on boys!

The difference between the two teams in the first leg was so clear that I almost had a stroke when I later saw we were 2-1 down. One more goal and we're out. Come on boys, I trust you, I love you, you can't do this to me, to all of us. I take a sip of whiskey from the bar. My throat is on fire but the kick is needed.

I check the time and the game should be finished by now. Clients are served so I take a deep breath and put the code into my phone, I swipe the screen and go to the BBC webpage. It finished 2-1 and Fulham are back in the play-off final. I throw my punch in the air, we made it, wow. With my heart pumping through my T-shirt I ecstatically move in and out the place. Diners look at me smiling and I return the smile. If they only knew.

As we shut, I text everybody I know. We are all delighted with the result; Jeff, Mark, the boys. We're again just a step away from the Premier League.

Local rivals Brentford beat Swansea in their semi-final and are the public's favourites to go up because of their stylish football and some really good players in their ranks, such as goal machine Ollie Watkins and Algerian superstar Saïd Benrahma among others.

But we are Fulham and showed during the campaign that we fear nobody.

It's 4 August and Lara is here. I'm torn. She flew over to see me and spend time together after more than a month and we're not going to see each other for a long time again after she leaves. At the same time I'd love to watch the boys and possibly celebrate! Damn.

Then I recall I wasn't able to watch the game even the last time so, a little superstitious and probably silly, I will not watch it this time.

The day at the beach is great and having the person you love next to you is superb. At night we have a restaurant booked. The food is okay, nothing to die for, and the view is great. And it's time to check the score.

Playing such a game in an empty Wembley should be illegal. Anyway, this is what we have to accept at present. It's an all-London affair and one of the teams will represent the west side of the capital city in the next Premier League season.

The Bees are favourites. They beat us twice, they play good football and they finished higher in the table. It's their 4-3-3 against our 4-2-3-1. Their top scorer Watkins, guiding the attack, our top scorer, Mitrović, on the bench as not 100 per cent fit.

I down the glass of wine, look at the sky and then at the phone. We've done it. WE ARE PREMIER LEAGUE!

I jump up and kiss Lara. She doesn't like football at all and she looks at me as if I just turned crazy. 'It's Fulham babe, you know the team I keep telling you I love up in London? Well, they got promoted to the English Serie A! You understand?!?!?!' 'Ah, football,' she replies, sipping her wine. 'No, not football my love, FULHAM, it's not just football,' I tell her.

After taking her to the airport I get home and watch the highlights. The win was totally deserved as during the 90 minutes Raya made a couple of good saves. In added time we could have won it if only Cavaleiro scored. Joe Bryan pulled that free kick invention out of nowhere so praise to him. A left-back scoring a double in a play-off final versus a local rival means hero status is forever almost assured.

I switch off the PC, open the door to the balcony and sit head up to the sun. I close my eyes and my mind goes straight to the fond memories I've got of Fulham beating Manchester United, running riot in Europe, and getting the scalp of many football giants. My heart pumps faster and a smile invades my face. We're going to be playing again in the Premier League, arguably the best league in the world by far. I can't wait to be back there and hopefully this will happen soon, albeit this Covid situation is getting more weird as the days go by.

I think about the day I'll eventually be able to be at Craven Cottage again. The excitement walking through Bishops Park and its lucky gates, fans singing, meat frying on the grill. The River Thames flowing calmly on the left while the lights start to take the scene in, the houses nearby and the majestic bridge shows its presence in the background.

The stadium floodlights adorning the sky in the distance, some kids imitating their idols on the grass, kicking a ball still too big for them yet too small compared to their dreams. The seller calling for the matchday programme while policemen on their horses patrol the crowd. Fans queuing in front of the gates chatting and guessing about today's game and then finally inside the most beautiful football ground in the whole earth. The boys in white coming out backed by the emphatic entrance music and that choir, the one you were born for, because I am Fulham, until I die.

Please don't take me home.

My Personal Lists

Favourite Fulham player since I've fallen in love with the club:

1. Clint Dempsey
2. Louis Saha
3. Bobby Zamora
4. Aleksandar Mitrović
5. Danny Murphy
6. Brede Hangeland
7. = Simon Davies, Heiðar Helguson, Tom Cairney, Claus Jensen

Best Fulham game attended live:

1. Fulham 4 Juventus 1, Europa League, 2010
2. Fulham 2 Hamburg 1, Europa League, 2010
3. Fulham 2 Wolfsburg 1, Europa League, 2010
4. Fulham 2 Shakhtar Donetsk 1, Europa League, 2010
5. Fulham 3 Manchester United 0, Premier League, 2009
6. Fulham 2 Wolves 0, Championship, 2018
7. Fulham 2 Birmingham 0, Premier League, 2008

Best manager:

1. Roy Hodgson
2. Slaviša Jokanović
3. Jean Tigana
4. Mark Hughes
5. Chris Coleman

6. Scott Parker
7. Kit Symons

Best Fulham kit:
1. Home 2007/08: LG
2. Home 2003–05: dabs.com
3. Home 2001/02: Pizza Hut
4. Home 2015/16: Visit Florida
5. Third 2009/10: LG
6. Away 2000/01: Demon
7. Away 2017/18: Grosvenor Casinos

Most hated opposing team:
1. Bolton and Blackburn managed by Sam Allardyce
2. Chelsea by José Mourinho
3. Tottenham
4. QPR and Cardiff by Neil Warnock
5. Wolves by Mick McCarthy

Most hated rival player:
1. John Terry – Chelsea
2. El Hadji Diouf – Bolton/Blackburn
3. Joey Barton – QPR/Newcastle
4. Tal Ben Haim – Bolton/Chelsea
5. Ed de Goey – Chelsea

Best opposing team seen live v Fulham:
1. Manchester City managed by Roberto Mancini
2. Manchester United with Cristiano Ronaldo
3. Arsenal managed by Arsène Wenger, 2005/06
4. Shatkhar Donetsk, Europa League, 2009/10
5. Atlético Madrid, Europa League, 2009/10

Best opponent player seen live:

1. Samir Nasri – Arsenal
2. Yaya Touré – Manchester City
3. David Silva – Manchester City
4. Cristiano Ronaldo – Manchester United
5. = Wayne Rooney (Manchester United), Thierry Henry (Arsenal), Carlos Tevez (Manchester United, Manchester City)

Best Fulham goal seen live:

1. Clint Dempsey v Juventus, Europa League, 2010
2. Simon Davies v Hamburg, Europa League, 2010
3. Paul Konchesky v West Ham, Premier League, 2009
4. Bobby Zamora v Shatkhar Donetsk, Europa League, 2010
5. Zoltán Gera v Manchester United, Premier League, 2009
6. Damien Duff v Birmingham City, Premier League, 2010
7. Bobby Zamora v Bolton Wanderers, Premier League, 2008

Best pub near Craven Cottage (past and present):

1. The Eight Bells
2. The Railway
3. The Rocket
4. The Duke's Head
5. The Spotted Horse

Acknowledgements

THANKS TO: My Mum and my whole family. My beloved nephews and Fulham supporters Manuel and Nicola, and also my "other nephews" Nicola Zane and Luca Zoppi. Lorenzo Tognon, Manuele Ruzzafante, Mirko Fiorasi and all other friends who joined me to the Cottage these years.

Mister Andrea Romano for allowing me into the Vicenza Women football, Giordano, Pietro and all the staff there. Obviously all the players of the Under 19 and the Primavera, I've learned a lot with you girls!

Gill Lavery and Leonardo Bonato, Vanessa Ghio and Alice Scoparin for keeping alive our memories of Giampaolo and Umberto.

All my good friends in the UK and especially Jeff, Mark and Ben, my Fulham Family.

My close friends Marco and Davide with whom I shared life in my first London days and also for being great friends together with their wives Cristina and Martina. Maika for always being there as a friend whenever I needed her. All the friends I grew up with, Mamo, Sea, Bega, Forcy, Alen among the others.

The Vanilla&Chocolate crazy gang in Mallorca: Mariano, Marcelo, Sebastian, Manu, Gaita, Maxi. Italy and Argentina are so connected.

Luigi, Marco, Nicola E. and Nicola N. and Simone, Rudy, Agnese, Roby Assi, and all the Italians in Mallorca. Mikel, my Northern Vicenza's brother. The one and only Mr.Cook.

Andy Cosentino for giving me tips about the book cover and running the NYC marathon by my side.

Jane and all the staff at Pitch Publishing.

And all others I've might forgotten, good or bad, thank you too for teaching me something inlife.

Andrea Ferretto for the cover picture.

Last but not least, all Fulham fans for supporting the best team in the World!

About the Author

Simone Abitante was born in Noventa Vicentina, on 1 November 1975. After struggling to get out of a technical high school he begun working as a barman and waiter. That brought him to live in the UK and Spain for several years, evolving into a maître d' and a sales manager. He eventually moved into coaching and personal growth and he's now back in Italy helping people and their investments. He's also a mental coach for the Vicenza Women Youth Academy. And he still absolutely loves Fulham regardless of the league they play in.